# TOGETHER THROUGH TIME

# Together Through Time

## *A Children's Guide to Cherishing Aging Parents*

MACK RAFEAL

UNIEK ENTERPRISES

# Contents

# INDEX

Introduction

4.3 Addressing common challenges in discussing sensitive topics with aging parents

## Chapter 5: Creating Cherished Memories
5.1 Encouraging children to spend quality time with their aging parents
5.2 Suggesting activities that foster connection and joy
5.3 Emphasizing the value of creating lasting memories

## Chapter 6: Navigating Challenges
6.1 Discussing common challenges that may arise in caring for aging parents
6.2 Providing guidance on problem-solving and conflict resolution
6.3 Encouraging resilience and patience in children

## Chapter 7: Balancing Responsibilities
7.1 Exploring the importance of balance in children's lives
7.2 Offering strategies for managing caregiving responsibilities alongside other commitments
7.3 Emphasizing the significance of self-care for children

## Chapter 8: Passing Down Values
8.1 Discussing the legacy of love, respect, and care
8.2 Highlighting the values and lessons children can pass down to future generations
8.3 Encouraging a sense of continuity and connection within the family

## Chapter 9:Conclusion
9.1 Summarizing key takeaways
9.2 Reinforcing the idea that cherishing aging parents is an ongoing, fulfilling journey
9.3 Inspiring children to embrace their role in creating a loving and supportive family environment.

# Introduction

In the endearing excursion of life, the ties that tight spot ages together structure the substance of family. "Together Through Time: A Youngsters' Manual for Loving Maturing Guardians" is a book that sets out on a strong investigation of the corresponding connection among kids and their maturing guardians. It dives into the obligations, delights, and difficulties that accompany the progression of time, encouraging a comprehension of the meaning of family bonds.

The underlying parts establish the groundwork for the book's focal subject, presenting the idea of maturing and its effect on guardians. Through age-fitting clarifications, youngsters are directed to grasp the regular course of becoming older. The account delicately addresses the difficulties looked by maturing people, imparting sympathy and empathy in youthful hearts. By introducing the repeating idea of life, the book lays out the interconnectedness of ages, underlining the essential jobs guardians play in shaping their youngsters' lives.

As the account unfurls, youngsters are delicately acquainted with their obligations and obligations toward their maturing guardians. Functional models represent the horde manners by which little thoughtful gestures can have a tremendous effect in the existences of maturing friends and family. The significance of successful correspondence turns into a point of convergence in the resulting part, directing youngsters on exploring discussions about touchy subjects with their maturing guardians. By stressing transparency and genuineness, the book furnishes youngsters with significant correspondence techniques.

The excursion of loving maturing guardians isn't just a bunch of liabilities; it's a valuable chance to make treasured recollections. The book urges youngsters to invest quality energy taking part in exercises that encourage association and euphoria. Through tales and ideas, it motivates a feeling of shared encounters that become enduring recollections, winding around an embroidery of affection and association.

However, this excursion isn't without its difficulties. The book truly addresses normal deterrents in focusing on maturing guardians, offering direction on critical thinking and compromise. It imparts flexibility and persistence, recognizing that the way of providing care might be requesting however is at last fulfilling.

A pivotal part of this guide lies in the investigation of equilibrium. It digs into the significance of offsetting providing care liabilities with different responsibilities in a youngster's life. The story urges kids to rehearse taking care of oneself, underscoring that a sound balance is crucial for both the kid and the maturing guardian.

In the end parts, the book takes an intelligent turn, investigating going down values through ages. It thinks about the tradition of adoration, regard, and mind that can be given over from guardians to kids. By highlighting the qualities and examples kids can grant to people in the future, the book builds up a feeling of congruity and association inside the family.

1. **Overview of the importance of family bonds**

   Family bonds structure the bedrock of human connections, giving a feeling of personality, having a place, and backing all through the different phases of life. In the perplexing snare of associations that comprise a family, the ties that tight spot ages together are especially significant. The significance of family bonds couldn't possibly be more significant, as they act as a wellspring of profound sustenance, flexibility, and shared encounters.

   At the center of these familial associations lies the idea of relationship — a shared dependence on each other for profound, monetary, and social help. Families offer a sanctuary of unqualified love and acknowledgment, furnishing people with a feeling that everything is good and steadiness. This emotionally supportive network turns out to be particularly urgent during testing times, filling in as a security net that pads the effect of life's unavoidable highs and lows.

   Family bonds assume a vital part in molding one's character and values. Since the beginning, people assimilate the social, moral, and moral structures inside the nuclear family. This common worth framework shapes the establishment for self-awareness and advancement, affecting direction, connections, and generally prosperity. The family turns into a storehouse of customs, customs, and stories that add to an aggregate feeling of history and coherence.

   All through the different life stages, family bonds go through unique changes. In youth, the family fills in as the essential wellspring of basic reassurance, direction, and socialization. As people change into youthfulness and adulthood, the family keeps on being a standard — a position of return and association in the midst of the difficulties of manufacturing one's own way. Once more, in later years, the elements shift, with the family frequently expecting a providing care job, especially with regards to maturing guardians.

The corresponding connection among kids and guardians, particularly as guardians age, is a topic that resounds profoundly in the texture of family bonds. It is inside this setting that the aide, "Together Through Time: A Kids' Manual for Esteeming Maturing Guardians," unfurls.

The story is woven with strings of liability, love, and association, meaning to impart in youngsters a comprehension of the significant obligation they hold in supporting and esteeming their maturing guardians.

As cultural designs advance and the elements of day to day life go through changes, the meaning of family bonds stays consistent. Families give a feeling of having a place in a quickly impacting world, encouraging a common character and reason. Besides, the basic encouragement got from family bonds adds to mental and profound prosperity, going about as a cushion against the burdens of current life.

Past the individual, family securities stretch out to the local area and society in general. Solid familial associations add to social union, making a gradually expanding influence that upgrades the general texture of networks. The qualities ingrained inside families frequently act as the structure blocks for dependable citizenship, compassion, and a feeling of aggregate liability.

With regards to "Together Through Time," the aide looks to support the significance of family bonds by focusing on a particular viewpoint — the connection among kids and their maturing guardians. It perceives the novel difficulties and prizes that accompany this specific period of day to day life, recognizing the mind boggling dance of providing care, understanding, and shared recollections that portray this excursion.

The aide urges youngsters to perceive the getting through force of familial bonds, underscoring that the obligations they embrace in focusing on their maturing guardians are obligations as well as articulations of affection and appreciation. It plans to give a guide to exploring the intricacies of this excursion with empathy, open correspondence, and a profound appreciation for the interesting jobs every relative plays.

In a world that frequently stresses independence and confidence, "Together Through Time" highlights the aggregate strength got from family bonds. It welcomes kids to see the difficulties of really focusing on maturing guardians not as weights but rather as any open doors to fortify these bonds and make a tradition of adoration and backing. At last, the aide support the possibility that family bonds are immortal and tough, equipped for enduring the everyday hardships and giving a wellspring of solace and association over the course of life's excursion.

2. **Introduction to the concept of aging and its impact on parents**

The certainty of maturing is an all inclusive part of the human experience, and its effect resounds significantly inside the familial setting. As people cross the different phases of life, the progression of time makes a permanent imprint, introducing both physical and inner difficulties. In the unpredictable embroidery of relational peculiarities, the idea of maturing presents a nuanced layer that requires grasping, sympathy, and variation.

The prologue to the idea of maturing inside the aide, "Together Through Time: A Kids' Manual for Valuing Maturing Guardians," fills in as a powerful investigation of this normal and unavoidable cycle. It recognizes the actual changes that go with maturing — turning gray hair, lines scratched by time, and changes in versatility. In any case, the story reaches out past the surface, digging into the close to home scene that maturing guardians explore.

Maturing carries with it a scope of feelings for guardians, from reflections on a daily routine very much experienced to worries about wellbeing, freedom, and the developing elements of familial connections. The aide carefully moves toward these intricacies, perceiving that maturing is definitely not a solitary encounter yet a diverse excursion that requires sympathy and understanding from relatives, especially youngsters.

The effect of maturing on guardians stretches out past the actual domain, enveloping mental and close to home aspects. The aide plans to cultivate a mindfulness among youngsters about the close to home subtleties that might go with maturing, like sensations of wistfulness, the clashing consciousness of life's fleetingness, and the longing for association and friendship. By sharpening kids to these close to home features, the aide establishes the groundwork for a more profound comprehension of their job in supporting and treasuring their maturing guardians.

In addition, the presentation establishes the vibe for the aide's emphasis on the corresponding idea of familial connections. It features the recurrent idea of life, where guardians who once offered relentless help and direction may now end up needing care and understanding. This repetitive viewpoint urges kids to see maturing not as a singular excursion but rather as a common encounter inside the nuclear family.

That's what the aide perceives, as guardians age, the jobs inside the family advance. It highlights the significance of adjusting to these progressions with elegance and awareness, encouraging a climate where the commitments of maturing guardians are esteemed and regarded. This affirmation of developing jobs turns into a foundation for the aide, outlining the resulting investigation of youngsters' liabilities and obligations toward their maturing guardians.

Basically, the prologue to the idea of maturing and its effect on guardians fills in as a sympathetic passage point into the aide's account. It welcomes kids to take part in a smart reflection on the certainty of maturing, recognizing the feelings and difficulties it brings for guardians. Thusly, the aide lays the preparation for a nuanced investigation of the proportional connection among youngsters and their maturing guardians — a relationship portrayed by adoration, obligation, and the common excursion through the progression of time.

The story urges youngsters to move toward the subject of maturing with responsiveness and open hearts, perceiving the excellence intrinsic in the various periods of life.

That's what it highlights, similarly as guardians assumed a necessary part in the early stages of their youngsters' lives, kids currently have the amazing chance to respond that consideration and backing as their folks age. This presentation turns into an impactful greeting for youngsters to leave on an excursion of figuring out, empathy, and loving the immortal association that ties ages together.

3. Setting the tone for the book's focus on children's responsibilities and duties towards their aging parents

Establishing the vibe for the aide, "Together Through Time: A Youngsters' Manual for Valuing Maturing Guardians," includes an intentional and insightful investigation of the obligations and obligations kids hold toward their maturing guardians. This tone-setting process is significant, as it establishes the groundwork for the aide's focal message — that really focusing on maturing guardians isn't simply a commitment yet a significant articulation of adoration, regard, and correspondence inside the nuclear family.

The aide attempts to move the point of view on youngsters' jobs from simple obligations to demonstrations of treasuring, underlining the significance of these obligations in supporting and supporting family bonds. It perceives that as guardians age, their requirements change, and youngsters are given a one of a kind chance to respond the consideration and backing they got in their early stages.

Integral to establishing this vibe is the possibility that these obligations are not difficult errands yet rather significant motions that add to the prosperity and satisfaction of maturing guardians. By outlining kids' jobs in this sure light, the aide empowers a mentality shift — from survey providing care as a commitment to moving toward it as a fundamental piece of the common familial excursion.

Besides, the aide recognizes that every family is extraordinary, and the particular obligations might differ in light of social, cultural, and individual elements. Establishing the vibe includes ingraining a feeling of adaptability, understanding that the idea of care and support can be different and versatile to the particular requirements and conditions of every family.

The tone-setting process likewise addresses the close to home part of providing care. It perceives that really focusing on maturing guardians includes actual undertakings as well as basic reassurance and friendship. The aide intends to pass that kids have the open door on to make significant associations with their maturing guardians during this period of life, encouraging a feeling of closeness and shared encounters.

Besides, the aide underlines the drawn out nature of these obligations, perceiving that the excursion of really focusing on maturing guardians is certainly not a one-time exertion yet a continuous responsibility. By establishing this vibe, kids are urged to see their jobs as consistent articulations of adoration and appreciation, making a feeling of congruity and association inside the family.

A urgent component in establishing the vibe is the investigation of open correspondence inside the family. The aide features the significance of discussing the difficulties and delights of really focusing on maturing guardians. This correspondence cultivates figuring out, compassion, and coordinated effort among relatives, building up the possibility that everybody assumes an imperative part in the aggregate prosperity of the family.

Moreover, establishing the vibe includes tending to possible worries or nerves kids might have about taking on providing care obligations. The aide means to reduce fears by giving direction on critical thinking, offering commonsense tips, and underscoring the encouraging groups of people accessible to youngsters as they explore this excursion.

The general tone tries to motivate a feeling of direction and satisfaction in kids as they embrace their parts in treasuring maturing guardians. It imparts that these obligations contribute not exclusively to the government assistance of guardians yet in addition to the reinforcing of familial bonds and the formation of a strong and cherishing family climate.

Fundamentally, establishing the vibe for the book's emphasis on kids' liabilities and obligations towards their maturing guardians is a nuanced cycle. It includes outlining these obligations as demonstrations of affection and valuing, perceiving the profound and pragmatic parts of providing care, and cultivating open correspondence inside the family. Thusly, the aide makes an establishment for youngsters to move toward the excursion of really focusing on maturing guardians with compassion, understanding, and a profound appreciation for the immortal associations that tight spot ages together.

# Chapter 1

Understanding Aging

Understanding maturing is a principal part of the aide, "Together Through Time: A Kids' Manual for Treasuring Maturing Guardians." It unfurls as a caring investigation, looking to furnish youngsters with age-fitting experiences into the normal and inescapable course of becoming older. This section fills in as a foundation for the whole aide, encouraging compassion, and supporting an underpinning of understanding that is fundamental for kids as they explore their parts in focusing on maturing guardians.

The investigation starts with a delicate prologue to the idea of maturing, recognizing its comprehensiveness and certainty. From a perspective of sympathy, the aide makes sense of that maturing is a characteristic movement that happens in everybody's life. By moving toward this point with responsiveness, the aide plans to disperse any expected feelings of trepidation or misinterpretations youngsters could have about the maturing system, developing a feeling of acknowledgment and understanding.

The aide then dives into the complex idea of maturing, enveloping the actual changes as well as the close to home and mental aspects. It portrays maturing, recognizing that it isn't just about wrinkles and turning gray hair yet in addition about the insight acquired, the encounters lived, and the tales that shape a singular's excursion. This approach intends to impart a profound appreciation for the wealth that accompanies a daily routine very much experienced.

To help with's how kids might interpret maturing, the aide uses age-fitting language and models. It utilizes engaging similitudes and correlations with convey complex thoughts in a way that reverberates with the formative phase of the youngster crowd. Thusly, the aide guarantees that youngsters can get a handle on the quintessence of maturing without feeling overpowered or confounded.

Integral to understanding maturing is the acknowledgment that it achieves a scope of encounters and feelings for people. The aide explores these close to home scenes, recognizing the wistfulness that might go with thinking back about the past, the insight acquired through life's illustrations, and the appreciation for the minutes that have molded one's presence. By investigating the profound aspects of maturing, the aide urges youngsters to understand their maturing guardians, perceiving the profundity and intricacy of their encounters.

Besides, the aide highlights that maturing is definitely not a uniform encounter; as different as the people go through it. Factors like wellbeing, way of life, and individual conditions add to extraordinary maturing ventures. This understanding fills in as an establishment for kids to move toward their folks' maturing cycle with responsiveness, perceiving that each parent might have particular requirements and viewpoints.

As the aide unfurls, it puts a specific accentuation on the job of youngsters in offering help and understanding during the maturing system. It imparts that kids have the ability to contribute decidedly to their folks' encounters of maturing by encouraging a climate of adoration, regard, and friendship. This change in context positions maturing not as a lone excursion but rather as a common family experience, building up the interconnectedness of ages.

Besides, the aide addresses the significance of encouraging an inspirational perspective towards maturing. It challenges cultural generalizations and urges youngsters to see maturing as a period of life that can be embraced with elegance and pride. By developing an inspirational perspective, kids are enabled to add to a strong and insisting climate for their maturing guardians, advancing profound prosperity.

Understanding maturing likewise includes recognizing the potential difficulties that might emerge. The aide tends to normal worries, for example, medical problems, changes in portability, and the developing elements of familial connections. By straightforwardly examining these difficulties, the aide furnishes kids with a reasonable point of view, setting them up to explore the intricacies of really focusing on maturing guardians with sympathy and strength.

Moreover, the aide features the significance of encouraging a feeling of organization and independence for maturing guardians. That's what it accentuates, while help is fundamental, regarding the independence and decisions of maturing guardians adds to their general prosperity. This understanding turns into a core value for kids as they explore their jobs, cultivating a climate that advances respect and freedom.

1.1 Age-appropriate explanation of the aging process

Exploring the complexities of the maturing system with kids requires a fragile and age-suitable methodology. "Together Through Time: A Kids' Manual for Treasuring Maturing Guardians" perceives the significance of giving youngsters an unmistakable and open clarification of the maturing system, custom-made to their formative stage. This part fills in as a scaffold between the calculated comprehension presented in the past section and the useful contemplations kids might experience as they take on liabilities toward their maturing guardians.

The aide starts by laying out a groundwork of information about the human existence cycle. It utilizes basic and interesting language to make sense of the idea of birth, development, and the normal movement of life. By securing the conversation in these natural ideas, the aide lays the foundation for youngsters to get a handle on the possibility that everybody goes through an excursion of maturing.

The subsequent stage includes presenting the thought that as individuals become older, their bodies go through changes. The aide utilizes age-fitting illustrations and relationships to make sense of these changes, making the data engaging and intelligible for youngsters. For example, it could compare the maturing system to the evolving seasons, where each season addresses an alternate stage throughout everyday life, complete with its one of a kind qualities and magnificence.

Vital to this age-proper clarification is the affirmation of the actual changes related with maturing. The aide acquaints youngsters with the possibility that similarly as they have encountered development achievements in their own lives, for example, figuring out how to walk or losing child teeth, grown-ups likewise go through changes as they age. These progressions could incorporate turning gray hair, the improvement of kinks, and a reduction in actual strength.

To upgrade understanding, the aide utilizes visual guides and models that resound with youngsters' encounters. By consolidating engaging situations, for example, the manner in which a most loved toy could give indications of mileage after some time, the aide works with an association between the natural and the idea of maturing. This approach demystifies the maturing system, making it not so much dynamic but rather more substantial for youngsters.

Significantly, the aide scatters any likely misinterpretations or fears kids might have about maturing. It stresses that maturing is a characteristic and ordinary piece of life, insisting that everybody, including guardians, goes through this excursion. By outlining maturing as a characteristic cycle instead of something to be dreaded, the aide encourages a positive and tolerating demeanor toward the real factors of becoming older.

As the clarification advances, the aide presents that while the body goes through changes, the embodiment of an individual — their character, recollections, and encounters — stays unaltered. This differentiation is vital in assisting youngsters with understanding that maturing doesn't decrease the center character of their folks. By featuring the coherence of the internal identity, the aide supports the persevering through association kids share with their maturing guardians.

The aide likewise recognizes that maturing carries with it an abundance of encounters and shrewdness. It urges youngsters to see their maturing guardians as supplies of information and stories, stressing the worth of these common accounts in making a feeling of family ancestry. This viewpoint welcomes kids to see their folks not exclusively from the perspective of actual changes but rather as people with a rich embroidery of encounters that add to the family's aggregate story.

Besides, the aide tends to the powerful idea of maturing, underscoring that everybody ages at their own speed. It presents the idea of changeability, making sense of that individuals age diversely founded on variables like hereditary qualities, way of life, and in general wellbeing. This understanding assists kids with valuing the uniqueness of their folks' maturing ventures, cultivating sympathy and an acknowledgment that there is nobody size-fits-all way to deal with maturing.

To build up the age-fitting clarification of the maturing system, the aide integrates intuitive components. It might incorporate exercises, like drawing or narrating, that permit youngsters to offer their viewpoints and sentiments about maturing. By drawing in youngsters in an innovative strategy, the aide supports the data introduced as well as gives an outlet to them to investigate their feelings and discernments.

Basically, the part on the age-fitting clarification of the maturing system fills in as a crucial extension between the calculated comprehension of maturing and the useful contemplations that kids will experience in their jobs as guardians.

By utilizing straightforward language, interesting models, and intelligent components, the aide guarantees that youngsters grasp the fundamental ideas of maturing as well as foster a positive and sympathetic mentality toward this normal and widespread part of the human experience.

1.2 Discussing common challenges faced by aging individuals

As the aide "Together Through Time: A Youngsters' Manual for Treasuring Maturing Guardians" unfurls, it perceives the significance of digging into the difficulties looked by maturing people. This section fills in as a significant component in giving kids a nuanced comprehension of the maturing system and sets them up for the intricacies they might experience as guardians to their maturing guardians.

The investigation starts with a compassionate affirmation that maturing frequently accompanies its arrangement of difficulties. By taking on a merciful tone, the aide intends to make a space for open discourse and understanding, permitting youngsters to explore the profound scene that might go with conversations about the challenges their folks could confront.

One of the essential difficulties examined in the aide is the actual part of maturing. It explains that as people become older, they might encounter a lessening in portability, changes in vision and hearing, and a general dialing back of physical processes. By furnishing kids with a reasonable comprehension of these actual changes, the aide prepares them to approach providing care liabilities with compassion and responsiveness.

The aide investigates the likely effect of constant medical issue that frequently go with maturing. It acquaints youngsters with normal circumstances like joint pain, diabetes, and coronary illness, making sense of them in age-proper terms. This data assists youngsters with embracing the truth that their folks could battle with wellbeing challenges, underlining the significance of offering help and understanding during these times.

Intently attached to actual difficulties is the aide's investigation of mental changes related with maturing. It delicately presents the idea that as individuals become older, they might encounter changes in memory and mental capability. By utilizing interesting models, for example, losing keys or neglecting names, the aide assists kids with understanding that these progressions are important for the typical maturing process.

Significantly, the aide stresses that these mental changes don't lessen the value or personality of maturing people. It urges kids to move toward these difficulties with persistence and understanding, encouraging a climate that esteems the individual past the limits forced by mental changes.

Besides, the aide tends to the potential close to home and mental difficulties that maturing people might experience. It examines sensations of depression, misfortune, or nervousness that can emerge because of changes in friendly associations, the deficiency of friends and family, or reflections on life advances. By investigating the close to home scene of maturing, the aide gets ready youngsters to give physical as well as everyday reassurance to their maturing guardians.

A focal subject in examining normal difficulties is the aide's accentuation on the significance of keeping up with freedom and poise for maturing guardians. It highlights that while help is fundamental, protecting the independence of maturing people adds to their general prosperity. This understanding turns into a core value for youngsters, empowering them to approach providing care liabilities with a regard for their folks' decisions and inclinations.

Monetary difficulties are additionally tended to in the aide, perceiving that maturing people might confront vulnerabilities connected with retirement, medical care costs, and other monetary contemplations. By acquainting youngsters with these real factors, the aide encourages an attention to the more extensive setting wherein their folks might explore their later years. This mindfulness turns into an establishment for youngsters to participate in open correspondence with their folks about monetary issues, offering help and help on a case by case basis.

One more test examined in the aide is the potential for changes in friendly associations and encouraging groups of people. It investigates the effect of retirement, the deficiency of companions or relatives, and the changing elements of social connections. By tending to these changes, the aide assists kids with figuring out the significance of cultivating a strong and comprehensive climate for their maturing guardians, moderating sensations of separation and dejection.

The aide likewise explores the intricacies of end-of-life contemplations. It urges kids to participate in open conversations with their folks about their desires in regards to medical care, living plans, and other significant choices. By tending to these subjects, the aide furnishes kids with a guide for moving toward delicate discussions and pursuing informed choices in a joint effort with their maturing guardians.

All through the conversation of normal difficulties, the aide stays aware of the close to home effect on kids. It perceives that recognizing these difficulties might summon a scope of feelings, including concern, bitterness, or tension. The aide urges youngsters to communicate their sentiments, encouraging a climate where open correspondence is esteemed. This accentuation on close to home prosperity turns into a vital piece of the aide's way to deal with planning youngsters for their jobs as guardians.

In outline, the section on examining normal difficulties looked by maturing people is a complete investigation that plans to furnish youngsters with a profound comprehension of the intricacies related with the maturing system. By tending to physical, mental, close to home, and monetary difficulties, the aide gives youngsters a comprehensive viewpoint. Besides, by underlining the significance of protecting freedom, poise, and open correspondence, the aide lays the basis for youngsters to move toward their providing care liabilities with sympathy, responsiveness, and a promise to supporting their maturing guardians through the different features of their excursions.

1.3 Encouraging empathy and compassion in children towards their aging parents

Empowering sympathy and sympathy in youngsters towards their maturing guardians is an essential part of the aide, "Together Through Time: A Kids' Manual for Loving Maturing Guardians." This section is a genuine investigation into encouraging a profound close to home association among kids and their maturing guardians, perceiving that compassion is the foundation of significant providing care.

The aide starts by characterizing compassion for youngsters in an open manner. It makes sense of that compassion includes understanding and talking about the thoughts of someone else. Utilizing appealing models, the aide assists kids with understanding the idea that compassion goes past compassion — it includes venturing into the shoes of their maturing guardians, perceiving their encounters, and answering with responsiveness.

Integral to empowering sympathy is the aide's accentuation on undivided attention. It acquaints youngsters with the specialty of listening with their ears as well as with their souls. By recognizing their folks' encounters, contemplations, and feelings, kids are urged to make a space for open correspondence. The aide gives commonsense tips to undivided attention, for example, keeping in touch, gesturing in understanding, and posing smart inquiries.

The aide additionally investigates the significance of approval in supporting compassion. It urges kids to approve their folks' sentiments and encounters, recognizing that everybody's process is remarkable. Thusly, kids figure out how to see the value in the wealth of their folks' lives and establish a climate where feelings are recognized and regarded.

To develop's comprehension kids might interpret their folks' encounters, the aide consolidates narrating. It might incorporate tales or accounts that catch the quintessence of maturing — accounts of flexibility, satisfaction, and the insight acquired throughout the long term. Through narrating, the aide develops a feeling of association and shared encounters, encouraging compassion by permitting kids to see the world through their folks' eyes.

Besides, the aide investigates the force of viewpoint taking. It urges youngsters to envision what exploring the physical and personal difficulties of aging may be like. By taking part in this creative activity, youngsters foster a feeling of compassion that rises above their own encounters, permitting them to see the value in the one of a kind points of view of their maturing guardians.

A vital part of empowering compassion is advancing a climate of profound security. The aide highlights the significance of making a space where kids feel happy with communicating their own feelings and concerns. By approving their sentiments, the aide assists kids with creating the capacity to understand people on a profound level, a fundamental part of compassionate providing care.

The aide likewise addresses possible feelings of dread or tensions that youngsters might hold onto about the maturing system. It gives age-suitable data about the real factors of maturing, dissipating misguided judgments, and normalizing the feelings that might emerge. By tending to these worries, the aide makes an establishment for kids to approach providing care with a feeling of serenity and understanding.

Critical to empowering sympathy is the aide's investigation of the correspondence intrinsic in familial connections. It conveys that similarly as guardians have shown sympathy and care all through a youngster's life, the opportunity arrives for kids to respond that affection and backing. This correspondence is outlined not as an obligation but rather as a characteristic expansion of the affection that ties families together, cultivating a feeling of shared liability.

In addition, the aide tends to the expected effect of cultural perspectives and generalizations about maturing on youngsters' discernments. It urges youngsters to challenge generalizations and perceive the distinction of their folks. Thusly, the aide engages kids to frame real associations in view of a profound comprehension of their folks' special characters, encounters, and desires.

As the investigation of sympathy unfurls, the aide consolidates exercises that effectively draw in kids in developing compassion. These exercises might incorporate pretending situations connected with maturing, partaking in intergenerational exercises, or making craftsmanship that communicates their sentiments and comprehension of their folks' encounters. These active encounters effectively support the aide's messages in a substantial and vital manner.

To supplement these exercises, the aide presents age-fitting writing and media that investigate subjects of sympathy, empathy, and intergenerational connections. By integrating assorted stories and points of view, the aide extends kids' points of view and urges them to see the value in the extravagance of the human experience across various ages.

The aide likewise perceives the significance of displaying sympathetic way of behaving. It supports guardians, teachers, and parental figures to represent sympathy in their connections with kids and maturing people. By seeing compassionate conduct in their good examples, youngsters are bound to assimilate these characteristics and coordinate them into their own providing care jobs.

Generally, the part on empowering sympathy and empathy in kids towards their maturing guardians is a genuine excursion into the profound center of providing care. By characterizing and representing sympathy, advancing undivided attention, approval, and point of view taking, the aide outfits kids with the close to home instruments expected to interface profoundly with their maturing guardians. It cultivates a climate of close to home wellbeing, scatters fears and generalizations, and supports correspondence inside the family. Through narrating, exercises, and openness to different viewpoints, the aide draws in youngsters in a groundbreaking investigation of sympathy that goes past comprehension to effectively embracing the delights and difficulties of maturing close by their folks.

# Chapter 2

The Circle of Life

The idea of the "Circle of Life" fills in as a focal subject in the aide, "Together Through Time: A Youngsters' Manual for Treasuring Maturing Guardians." This part is a strong investigation that rises above the straight movement of time, welcoming kids to see life as a recurrent excursion where each stage holds its exceptional excellence and importance. From the perspective of the Circle of Life, the aide enlightens the interconnectedness of ages and the persevering through bonds that wind through the texture of family.

At its center, the Circle of Life typifies the repetitive idea of presence — the nonstop stream from birth to development, maturing, and ultimately passing on. The aide acquaints youngsters with this idea by drawing matches between the times of nature and the various phases of human existence. It lays out a figurative system that reverberates with kids, assisting them with conceptualizing life's excursion as a consistently turning circle.

The aide utilizes age-suitable language and representations to delineate the interconnectedness of family connections inside the Circle of Life. It makes sense of that, similarly as guardians assume an imperative part in the beginning phases of a youngster's life, kids, thusly, become guardians and mates as their folks age.

This interconnectedness is portrayed as a corresponding dance, stressing that every individual from the family adds to the prosperity and congruity of the entirety.

Through the illustration of the Circle of Life, the aide tends to the certainty of maturing and the progression of time. It cultivates a comprehension that, similar as the evolving seasons, life advances through various stages, each with its extraordinary attributes. By embracing this cyclic viewpoint, youngsters are urged to see the value in the transient idea of every second and perceive the excellence inborn in the developing embroidered artwork of day to day life.

The aide likewise investigates the possibility that, inside the Circle of Life, maturing is definitely not a singular excursion yet a common encounter inside the nuclear family. It stresses the meaning of family bonds as a wellspring of solidarity and backing over the course of life's excursion. This point of view welcomes youngsters to move toward the maturing system with a feeling of solidarity and cooperation, perceiving that they are important for a bigger familial story.

Essential to the investigation of the Circle of Life is the aide's accentuation on the qualities and illustrations went down through ages. That's what it conveys, similarly as guardians bestowed shrewdness and direction during a kid's early stages, youngsters presently have the potential chance to add to the family heritage. This passing down of values turns into a string that winds through the Circle of Life, interfacing past, present, and people in the future.

The aide consolidates narrating as an amazing asset to show the idea of the Circle of Life. It might incorporate stories that range ages, exhibiting the versatility, love, and shared encounters that characterize everyday life. Through these accounts, youngsters are welcome to interface with the more extensive story of their family, encouraging a feeling of progression and association that reaches out past individual lifetimes.

Furthermore, the aide investigates the job of ceremonies and customs inside the Circle of Life. It urges families to make significant ceremonies that celebrate achievements, honor recollections, and fortify familial securities. These customs become representative markers inside the circle, meaning the interconnectedness of ages and the getting through nature of family ties.

The investigation of the Circle of Life stretches out to the possibility of heritage — the engraving that people leave on their families and networks. The aide urges youngsters to think about the tradition of affection, strength, and values passed somewhere around their folks. By perceiving the effect of their folks' commitments, kids gain a more profound appreciation for their job inside the Circle of Life.

Also, the aide tends to the transient idea of life and the significance of treasuring every second inside the Circle of Life. It stresses the benefit of investing quality energy with maturing guardians, participating in significant discussions, and making enduring recollections. This point of view urges youngsters to approach providing care as a chance to add to the wealth of their folks' lives and reinforce the bonds inside the family circle.

The aide additionally addresses the idea of interconnectedness past the nuclear family. It investigates the more extensive local area and cultural setting inside the Circle of Life, perceiving that people assume parts inside their families as well as inside the bigger human experience. This extended point of view urges youngsters to see their obligations toward maturing guardians as a feature of an aggregate work to make an empathetic and steady society.

As the aide unfurls the idea of the Circle of Life, it tends to expected difficulties and vulnerabilities that might emerge. It perceives that life's process is set apart by both delights and distresses, triumphs and difficulties. By recognizing these real factors, the aide plans youngsters to explore the intricacies of providing care with strength and a profound appreciation for the recurring pattern of the Circle of Life.

Basically, the part on the Circle of Life is a significant investigation that rises above the straight movement of time, welcoming kids to embrace life as a persistent and interconnected venture. Through the representation of the Circle of Life, the aide ingrains a feeling of solidarity, congruity, and shared liability inside the family. It urges youngsters to see maturing not as a single encounter but rather as a mutual dance where every part assumes a crucial part in the continuous story of day to day life. This point of view encourages a profound appreciation for the excellence inborn in the recurrent idea of presence and enables youngsters to explore their jobs as parental figures with adoration, empathy, and a significant comprehension of the getting through bonds that interface ages inside the Circle of Life.

### 2.1 Exploring the interconnectedness of generations

Investigating the interconnectedness of ages is a significant excursion inside the aide, "Together Through Time: A Youngsters' Manual for Treasuring Maturing Guardians." This section digs into the complex trap of connections that tight spot grandparents, guardians, and kids, stressing that the strings of association stretch out across time, molding the aggregate story of the family.

The investigation starts by recognizing the verifiable and social setting that adds to the interconnectedness of ages. The aide perceives that family customs, values, and stories are much of the time elapsed as the years progressed, making a common heritage that joins grandparents, guardians, and youngsters.

By understanding this continuum, youngsters are urged to see the value in the profundity of their familial roots and the lavishness that comes from being important for a generational embroidery.

A focal topic in investigating interconnectedness is the idea of family customs. The aide acquaints youngsters with the possibility that specific practices, festivities, and customs are given over starting with one age then onto the next. Whether it's an exceptional occasion dinner, a loved family custom, or a remarkable approach to praising achievements, these practices become strings that wind through time, interfacing relatives across ages.

In addition, the aide investigates the job of narrating in sending the encounters and shrewdness of more seasoned ages to more youthful ones. It underscores that grandparents, specifically, act as narrators, sharing accounts, recollections, and life examples. Through these stories, youngsters gain a more profound comprehension of their family's ancestry, producing an association with the past that shapes their present and future.

To represent the force of narrating, the aide might integrate age-suitable family stories or folktales that convey immortal subjects and values. This story approach draws in youngsters in a spellbinding investigation of their social legacy, cultivating a deep satisfaction and association with the bigger human experience across ages.

The aide likewise features the impact of good examples inside the family. It underscores that grandparents, guardians, and, surprisingly, more established kin act as good examples, molding the qualities and ways of behaving of more youthful relatives. By investigating the positive characteristics displayed by more seasoned ages, youngsters are urged to consider themselves to be essential for a tradition of solidarity, strength, and sympathy.

From the perspective of interconnectedness, the aide tends to the unique idea of family jobs. That's what it perceives, as youngsters develop, their jobs inside the family advance. The aide energizes an appreciation for the recurrent idea of these jobs — where youngsters, once focused on, become guardians in the later phases of life. This mindfulness encourages a feeling of correspondence and shared liability inside the nuclear family.

The investigation of interconnectedness reaches out past the close family to the more extensive local area. The aide underscores that families are essential for bigger interpersonal organizations, and the associations shaped inside these organizations add to a feeling of aggregate help. By perceiving the interchange between family, local area, and cultural impacts, kids foster a comprehension of their place inside the more extensive snare of connections.

Significantly, the aide investigates the idea of generational insight. It imparts that every age brings an extraordinary viewpoint, molded by its encounters, difficulties, and wins. By valuing the different experiences presented by various ages, kids gain a more extensive comprehension of the world, cultivating a feeling of inclusivity and receptiveness.

The aide additionally addresses likely generational holes or contrasts in viewpoints. It supports open correspondence and shared regard, perceiving that generational variety enhances everyday life. By exploring these distinctions with compassion, kids figure out how to see the value in the worth of different perspectives and encounters inside the interconnected snare of ages.

Moreover, the aide investigates the profound bonds that rise above time inside the family. It dives into the profound love, care, and feeling of having a place that portray familial connections. By recognizing the close to home underpinnings of interconnectedness, youngsters are urged to move toward their jobs as guardians with a heart loaded with empathy and a pledge to supporting the profound prosperity of their maturing guardians.

A critical part of investigating interconnectedness is perceiving the congruity of affection inside the family. The aide conveys that affection is an immortal string that winds through the ages, making a feeling of congruity and association. By understanding the persevering through nature of familial love, youngsters are engaged to move toward their providing care jobs with a significant appreciation for the profound bonds that endure everyday hardship.

To improve the investigation of interconnectedness, the aide consolidates intelligent components. It might incorporate exercises that include talking with grandparents, making a genealogy, or partaking in intergenerational projects. These exercises build up the data introduced as well as give youngsters active encounters that extend their association with their family's ancestry.

The aide likewise perceives the job of grandparents as dynamic supporters of the relational peculiarity. It accentuates the significance of esteeming the encounters, viewpoints, and commitments of grandparents. By cultivating a feeling of inclusivity and regard, youngsters figure out how to embrace the extraordinary job that grandparents play in molding the interconnected story of the family.

Furthermore, the aide investigates the idea of the "sandwich age," perceiving that a few people might wind up at the same time focusing on maturing guardians and supporting their own kids. By tending to the difficulties and awards of being essential for the sandwich age, the aide outfits youngsters with a comprehension of the intricacies that might emerge inside the interconnected trap of family connections.

Generally, the section on investigating the interconnectedness of ages is a significant excursion into the core of familial connections. By diving into family customs, narrating, good examples, and generational insight, the aide lays out a distinctive representation of the strings that interface grandparents, guardians, and youngsters across time. It stresses the unique idea of family jobs, the impact of more extensive interpersonal organizations, and the getting through force of affection inside the interconnected trap of ages. Through drawing in exercises and an appreciation for the different viewpoints inside the family, the aide enables kids to explore their jobs as parental figures with a profound feeling of association, regard, and a promise to saving the immortal securities that connect ages together.

### 2.2 Highlighting the roles parents played in children's lives

Featuring the jobs guardians played in kids' lives is an intelligent excursion inside the aide, "Together Through Time: A Youngsters' Manual for Treasuring Maturing Guardians." This section is a recognition for the multi-layered jobs guardians expect in supporting, directing, and significantly shaping the existences of their youngsters. By analyzing the urgent jobs guardians play, the aide respects the commitments of guardians as well as makes way for youngsters to respond these jobs as their folks age.

At the core of this investigation is the basic job of providing care that guardians embrace from the second a youngster is conceived. The aide recognizes the sacrificial demonstrations of supporting, taking care of, and giving a protected and cherishing climate for newborn children. By highlighting the meaning of early providing care, the aide lays the foundation for youngsters to see the value in the progression of care and backing as their folks enter another period of life.

The aide dives into the job of training and direction that guardians give all through a kid's early stages. It perceives guardians as the primary educators, giving scholarly information as well as essential fundamental abilities, values, and social insight. By featuring the job of guardians as instructors, the aide urges youngsters to perceive the wealth of the information passed down and the significance of proceeding with this inheritance inside the family.

As youngsters develop, guardians expect the job of tutors and good examples. The aide investigates the impact of parental direction in forming youngsters' goals, values, and character. It stresses that guardians act as living models, displaying ways of behaving, morals, and perspectives that add to the moral and profound improvement of their youngsters. This acknowledgment makes way for kids to move toward their providing care jobs with a profound comprehension of the effect parental direction has on significantly shaping lives.

The aide further investigates the job of basic reassurance and friendship that guardians give. It recognizes the solace, support, and understanding guardians offer during seasons of delight, misery, or vulnerability. By featuring the close to home bonds fashioned among guardians and kids, the aide encourages an appreciation for the significant effect of consistent reassurance, establishing the groundwork for youngsters to respond these feelings as their folks age.

Also, the aide perceives the job of guardians as suppliers and overseers. It tends to the penances and difficult work guardians put resources into guaranteeing the prosperity and solidness of their families. By recognizing the supplier job, the aide imparts in youngsters a feeling of appreciation for the endeavors made by their folks and a comprehension of the obligations that accompany providing care.

Critical to the investigation of parental jobs is the acknowledgment of the penances guardians make for their kids. The aide digs into the magnanimity intrinsic in life as a parent — the late evenings, the monetary speculations, and the endless choices made with the prosperity of the kid as a main priority. By featuring these penances, the aide imparts in kids a profound feeling of appreciation for the getting through affection and responsibility that guardians bring to their jobs.

Additionally, the aide investigates the job of guardians as planners of family customs and social personality. It perceives that guardians make light of a focal job in passing social practices, customs, and values that add to the texture of everyday life. By underscoring the significance of social progression, the aide welcomes youngsters to esteem and protect the social legacy woven into their familial embroidered artwork.

The investigation of parental jobs reaches out to guardians as promoters and defenders. It recognizes the promotion guardians embrace for their youngsters' prosperity, whether it's exploring the schooling system, tending to medical care needs, or guaranteeing a safe and sustaining climate. By perceiving guardians as supporters, the aide engages youngsters to advocate for and safeguard their maturing guardians as they face new difficulties.

As the aide unfurls, it tends to the unique idea of nurturing jobs as youngsters change into immaturity and adulthood. It perceives the developing relationship elements, where guardians become parental figures as well as confided in comrades and partners. By investigating the evolving elements, the aide encourages a comprehension of the equal idea of parent-kid connections, getting ready youngsters to embrace their jobs as guardians with sympathy and joint effort.

Critically, the aide digs into the idea of unrestricted love that guardians present to their youngsters. It perceives the resolute help, acknowledgment, and love that guardians offer, paying little mind to conditions or difficulties.

By stressing the profundity of parental love, the aide lays the basis for youngsters to move toward their jobs as guardians with a significant comprehension of the persevering through nature of familial securities.

To improve the investigation of parental jobs, the aide consolidates individual tales, tributes, and reflections from people who share their encounters of the effective jobs their folks played in their lives. By consolidating different points of view, the aide makes a mosaic of stories that reverberate with the changed ways guardians add to the existences of their youngsters.

The aide likewise investigates the tradition of flexibility and strength that guardians pass down to their kids. It perceives that guardians frequently explore difficulties, misfortunes, and wins, filling in as models of flexibility and determination. By featuring the tradition of solidarity, the aide rouses kids to move toward the providing care venture with a feeling of versatility and a pledge to exploring difficulties with elegance and assurance.

Besides, the aide tends to the significance of open correspondence in parent-youngster connections. It perceives that compelling correspondence is a crucial part of nurturing jobs, empowering figuring out, co-ordinated effort, and the sharing of encounters. By stressing the worth of open correspondence, the aide urges youngsters to participate in significant discussions with their maturing guardians, cultivating a more profound association and understanding.

In investigating parental jobs, the aide perceives the impact of fathers and moms as remarkable supporters of the relational peculiarity. It recognizes the different manners by which fathers and moms support, guide, and deeply influence the existences of their youngsters. By perceiving the particular however reciprocal jobs of fathers and moms, the aide praises the wealth that comes from the remarkable commitments of the two guardians.

The aide likewise addresses the idea of parent-kid bonds as long lasting associations that rise above time. That's what it perceives, even as kids become grown-ups, the bonds framed with their folks stay an essential part of their personalities. By investigating the persevering through nature of parent-kid bonds, the aide imparts in youngsters a feeling of congruity and association that reaches out past the various periods of life.

2.3 Emphasizing the cyclical nature of care and support within a family

Stressing the repetitive idea of care and backing inside a family is a focal subject in the aide, "Together Through Time: A Youngsters' Manual for Treasuring Maturing Guardians." This part welcomes kids to consider the interconnectedness of providing care, perceiving that the jobs of parental figures and mind beneficiaries develop over the long haul. By featuring the repeating idea of care and backing, the aide gives a structure to kids to grasp their jobs as guardians to maturing guardians inside the more extensive setting of familial connections.

At the center of this investigation is the acknowledgment that the providing care venture is definitely not a single direction road yet rather a repeating cycle that unfurls inside the nuclear family. The aide urges kids to think about the consideration and backing they got in their early stages, stressing the jobs played by guardians, grandparents, and other relatives. By recognizing the consideration presented to them, kids gain an appreciation for the repeating trade of affection and backing inside the family.

The aide dives into the beginning phases of providing care inside the family, where guardians accept the essential job of parental figures to their kids. It highlights the sacrificial demonstrations of sustaining, giving, and safeguarding that guardians embrace from early stages through pre-adulthood. By stressing this underlying period of providing care, the aide makes way for kids to perceive the repeating idea of care, establishing the groundwork for their own jobs as guardians as their folks age.

Besides, the aide investigates the correspondence intrinsic in familial connections. It imparts that the consideration and support kids get in their initial years make an underpinning of affection and security that turns into a wellspring for corresponding providing care in later stages. By perceiving the repetitive idea of providing care, the aide welcomes youngsters to move toward their jobs as parental figures with a feeling of congruity, appreciation, and a comprehension of the persevering through bonds that connect ages inside a family.

The investigation of the repetitive idea of care stretches out to the possibility of grandparents assuming urgent parts in providing care. The aide accentuates the remarkable commitments of grandparents in giving insight, direction, and consistent reassurance. By featuring the jobs played by grandparents in the family providing care dynamic, the aide encourages an appreciation for the multi-generational trade of care and backing inside the nuclear family.

As the aide unfurls, it tends to the change of providing care jobs as kids mature into grown-ups. It perceives that the recurrent idea of care includes a shift from getting care to effectively giving consideration. By recognizing this change, the aide gets ready youngsters for their jobs as guardians to maturing guardians, accentuating the significance of moving toward this stage with sympathy, empathy, and a comprehension of the developing elements inside the family.

The aide investigates the idea of the "sandwich age," recognizing that a few people end up all the while really focusing on maturing guardians and supporting their own youngsters. By perceiving the difficulties and obligations related with being essential for the sandwich age, the aide gives a nuanced comprehension of the complicated interchange between providing care jobs and the repeating idea of family care.

Vital to the investigation of the repetitive idea of care is the affirmation of the developing requirements of maturing guardians. The aide addresses the physical, close to home, and reasonable contemplations that accompany maturing, underscoring that the consideration gave to maturing guardians is a characteristic expansion of the consideration and backing guardians once offered their youngsters. By perceiving the developing necessities of maturing guardians, the aide gets ready kids to explore the intricacies of providing care with responsiveness and a pledge to safeguarding their folks' prosperity.

Moreover, the aide highlights the meaning of open correspondence inside the family. It urges youngsters to take part in fair and empathetic discussions with their maturing guardians about their necessities, inclinations, and wants. By cultivating open correspondence, the aide guarantees that the repeating idea of care is portrayed by common grasping, coordinated effort, and a common obligation to the prosperity of all relatives.

The investigation of the repeating idea of care consolidates the idea of "guardian correspondence." The aide imparts that the consideration given by youngsters to their maturing guardians isn't simply an obligation however an equal trade of affection, regard, and backing. By outlining providing care as a cooperative undertaking, the aide cultivates a feeling of shared liability and solidarity inside the family.

In addition, the aide recognizes the close to home scene of providing care. It perceives that providing care includes a scope of feelings, including love, happiness, challenges, and here and there, distress. By tending to the close to home intricacies, the aide gives youngsters devices to explore the providing care venture with versatility, sympathy, and a profound appreciation for the repetitive idea of feelings inside familial connections.

To improve the investigation of the repetitive idea of care, the aide might consolidate individual stories, tributes, and reflections from people who have encountered the powerful trade of care inside their families. These genuine accounts give nuanced experiences into the difficulties and prizes of providing care, featuring the repetitive idea of adoration and backing that winds through family stories.

The aide likewise investigates the idea of heritage inside the repeating idea of care. It conveys that the consideration gave to maturing guardians turns out to be essential for the family inheritance — a demonstration of the getting through bonds and values went down through ages. By perceiving the tradition of care, the aide motivates youngsters to move toward their jobs as guardians with a deep satisfaction, appreciation, and a pledge to protecting the familial tradition of affection and backing.

The repeating idea of care is additionally accentuated through the idea of "family ceremonies." The aide urges families to make significant customs that celebrate achievements, honor recollections, and fortify familial securities. These ceremonies become emblematic markers inside the recurrent excursion of providing care, cultivating a feeling of progression and association that rises above individual lifetimes.

Critically, the aide tends to the likely difficulties and vulnerabilities related with providing care. It perceives that the recurrent idea of care includes exploring both delights and distresses, victories and misfortunes. By recognizing these real factors, the aide plans youngsters to move toward their jobs as guardians with flexibility, versatility, and a profound comprehension of the repetitive idea of life's excursion.

Fundamentally, the section on underlining the recurrent idea of care and backing inside a family is an intelligent investigation into the interconnectedness of providing care jobs inside the familial embroidery. By looking at the jobs of guardians, grandparents, and youngsters in the repetitive trade of care, the aide furnishes kids with a system to comprehend and value their developing jobs as parental figures to maturing guardians. This investigation highlights the getting through nature of familial bonds, the correspondence innate in providing care, and the significance of moving toward the providing care venture with sympathy, empathy, and a significant comprehension of the repetitive idea of adoration and backing inside the family.

# Chapter 3

Responsibilities and Duties

Diving into the multifaceted snare of familial connections, the aide, "Together Through Time: A Youngsters' Manual for Loving Maturing Guardians," investigates the significant feeling of Liabilities and Obligations that kids embrace as their folks age. This part fills in as a compass, directing kids through the intricacies of providing care, disclosing the multi-layered jobs and obligations they embrace to guarantee the prosperity, respect, and satisfaction of their maturing guardians.

At the core of this investigation is the affirmation of providing care as a holy obligation, a characteristic expansion of the affection and backing youngsters got in their early stages. The aide highlights that Obligations and Obligations go past simple errands; they incorporate a promise to protecting the poise, freedom, and personal satisfaction of maturing guardians.

The aide starts by investigating the down to earth parts of providing care, tending to the actual necessities of maturing guardians. It digs into undertakings, for example, helping with everyday exercises, overseeing medical services needs, and guaranteeing a protected and open to living climate. By giving reasonable direction, the aide outfits youngsters with the abilities and information expected to satisfy their obligations such that regards the independence and inclinations of their maturing guardians.

As the investigation unfurls, the aide accentuates the significance of daily encouragement in providing care. It perceives that Obligations and Obligations reach out to giving friendship, sympathy, and a listening ear to maturing guardians who might be exploring the profound intricacies of the maturing system. By tending to the profound scene of providing care, the aide plans youngsters to satisfy their obligations with a profound comprehension of the all encompassing necessities of their folks.

In addition, the aide investigates the idea of dynamic inside the providing care dynamic. It perceives that youngsters might have to settle on choices for the benefit of their maturing guardians, taking into account their wellbeing and inclinations. By tending to the obligations related with independent direction, the aide enables youngsters to explore these complicated decisions with responsiveness, open correspondence, and a promise to maintaining their folks' desires.

Significant to the conversation of Obligations and Obligations is the investigation of monetary contemplations in providing care. The aide perceives that overseeing funds, medical services costs, and lawful issues might become vital parts of providing care liabilities. By giving direction on these viable perspectives, the aide guarantees that kids can explore the monetary intricacies of providing care with straightforwardness, obligation, and a pledge to getting their folks' prosperity.

The aide likewise addresses the idea of pushing for maturing guardians inside the medical care framework. It perceives that youngsters might should major areas of strength for be, guaranteeing that their folks get suitable clinical consideration, backing, and consideration. By tending to the support job, the aide engages youngsters to explore the medical services scene with self-assuredness, information, and a profound obligation to protecting the wellbeing and nobility of their folks.

The investigation of Obligations and Obligations stretches out to the personal difficulties related with seeing the maturing system. The aide recognizes that youngsters might encounter a scope of feelings, including pain, dread, and vulnerability, as they witness their folks age. By tending to these close to home intricacies, the aide furnishes youngsters with devices to explore their sentiments with versatility, compassion, and a guarantee to supporting the profound prosperity of their maturing guardians.

Moreover, the aide perceives the possible effect of social, cultural, and familial assumptions on kids' view of their Obligations and Obligations. It urges youngsters to consider their qualities, convictions, and the special elements of their family, perceiving that providing care is a profoundly private excursion formed by individual conditions and social settings. By tending to these impacts, the aide engages kids to move toward their obligations with a feeling of validness, social responsiveness, and a promise to regarding their family's interesting elements.

A critical part of Liabilities and Obligations is the investigation of using time effectively and taking care of oneself for guardians. The aide recognizes that providing care can be requesting and tedious, and youngsters might end up shuffling numerous obligations. By giving direction on using time effectively and the significance of taking care of oneself, the aide guarantees that youngsters can satisfy their obligations without undermining their prosperity.

The aide additionally investigates the idea of defining limits inside the providing care relationship. It perceives that kids might have to offset their obligations with their very own and proficient lives. By tending to the significance of defining limits, the aide urges youngsters to lay out a providing care system that is feasible, conscious, and helpful for keeping up with their own wellbeing and balance.

The investigation of Obligations and Obligations envelops the idea of open correspondence inside the family. The aide underlines that viable correspondence is essential to satisfying providing care liabilities, taking into account coordinated effort, understanding, and the sharing of points of view. By encouraging open correspondence, the aide guarantees that youngsters can explore their jobs with straightforwardness, sympathy, and a pledge to keeping up major areas of strength for with bonds.

Furthermore, the aide tends to the potential difficulties related with kin elements in providing care. It perceives that kin might have fluctuating points of view, obligations, and ways to deal with providing care. By recognizing the intricacies of kin connections, the aide gives direction on cultivating joint effort, settling clashes, and guaranteeing that providing care liabilities are shared fairly.

Significant to the investigation of Obligations and Obligations is the acknowledgment of the repeating idea of care inside the family. The aide underlines that youngsters, when beneficiaries of care, presently have the chance to respond that consideration to their maturing guardians. By outlining providing care as a characteristic expansion of the adoration and backing got in before phases of life, the aide imparts in youngsters a feeling of obligation that is established in appreciation, regard, and a guarantee to protecting the familial bonds that interface ages.

The aide likewise investigates the possible effect of cultural assumptions and generalizations on youngsters' impression of their providing care liabilities. It urges youngsters to challenge generalizations, embrace the variety of providing care jobs, and perceive the interesting qualities and commitments they bring to the providing care dynamic. By tending to cultural impacts, the aide engages youngsters to move toward their obligations with legitimacy, flexibility, and a promise to rethinking providing care inside the setting of their family's qualities.

Besides, the aide underscores the idea of correspondence inside the family. It imparts that the consideration and support youngsters give to their maturing guardians are obligations as well as an equal trade of affection, regard, and appreciation. By outlining providing care as a cooperative undertaking, the aide encourages a feeling of shared liability and solidarity inside the nuclear family.

The investigation of Obligations and Obligations consolidates the possibility of heritage inside the providing care venture. The aide perceives that the consideration gave to maturing guardians turns out to be important for the family heritage — a demonstration of the persevering through bonds and values went down through ages. By recognizing the tradition of care, the aide moves kids to move toward their jobs with a deep satisfaction, appreciation, and a promise to protecting the familial tradition of adoration and backing.

Fundamentally, the section on Liabilities and Obligations is a significant investigation into the complicated embroidery of providing care inside the family. By tending to reasonable viewpoints, close to home intricacies, and the more extensive cultural effects on providing care liabilities, the aide furnishes kids with the information and outlook expected to satisfy their obligations with credibility, empathy, and a profound obligation to safeguarding the prosperity and pride of their maturing guardians. This investigation highlights the all encompassing nature of providing care, underscoring that Obligations and Obligations are errands as well as a holy responsibility that moves through the repeating excursion of familial connections.

3.1 Identifying specific duties children can undertake to support aging parents

Inside the empathetic aide, "Together Through Time: A Youngsters' Manual for Valuing Maturing Guardians," the section zeroing in on "Distinguishing Explicit Obligations" uncovers a commonsense guide for kids exploring the obligations of providing care for their maturing guardians. This investigation dives into substantial and significant ways kids can uphold their folks, guaranteeing their prosperity, solace, and poise during the later phases of life.

At the center of this section is the acknowledgment that providing care includes a range of liabilities, both profound and pragmatic. The aide stresses that recognizing explicit obligations requires a nuanced comprehension of the interesting necessities and inclinations of maturing guardians, encouraging a climate of care that is custom fitted to their singular conditions.

Functional providing care obligations become the dominant focal point in the investigation, starting with aiding everyday exercises. The aide perceives that maturing might get difficulties performing routine undertakings, and kids can assume a vital part in offering help. This incorporates helping with exercises like feast arrangement, housekeeping, and individual consideration, guaranteeing that guardians can explore their regular routines effortlessly and nobility.

The aide digs into medical services related obligations, recognizing that overseeing clinical necessities is a critical part of providing care. Kids might embrace liabilities like going with guardians to clinical arrangements, sorting out prescriptions, and liaising with medical services experts to guarantee thorough and facilitated care. By tending to medical care obligations, the aide engages kids to effectively take part in shielding their folks' actual prosperity.

Besides, the investigation stretches out to the close to home prosperity of maturing guardians. The aide perceives the significance of giving friendship and consistent encouragement, particularly as guardians explore the intricacies of maturing. Kids might embrace obligations like taking part in significant discussions, taking an interest in shared exercises, and offering a listening ear. By tending to close to home requirements, the aide guarantees that youngsters can add to their folks' satisfaction and profound versatility.

Furthermore, the aide investigates the idea of establishing a protected and happy with living climate for maturing guardians. This implies recognizing and tending to likely perils, guaranteeing openness inside the home, and making adjustments to help autonomous residing. By tending to natural contemplations, the aide outfits youngsters with the information to make a space that advances their folks' security and prosperity.

The investigation of explicit obligations incorporates monetary obligations related with providing care. The aide perceives that overseeing funds, planning, and tending to lawful issues might become basic parts of providing care obligations. By giving direction on monetary contemplations, the aide guarantees that kids can explore these obligations with straightforwardness, obligation, and a pledge to getting their folks' monetary prosperity.

The idea of dynamic inside the providing care dynamic is likewise tended to. Kids might end up engaged with choices connected with medical care, legitimate issues, and different parts of their folks' lives. The aide enables kids to move toward decision-production with sympathy, regard for their folks' independence, and a pledge to maintaining their desires.

Significant to the investigation of explicit obligations is the acknowledgment of the different necessities of maturing guardians. The aide urges youngsters to tailor their providing care approach in light of the remarkable conditions, inclinations, and social contemplations of their folks. By recognizing the singularity of providing care needs, the aide guarantees that kids can offer help that is delicate, customized, and deferential.

In addition, the aide perceives the significance of open correspondence inside the providing care relationship. Kids might have to participate in legitimate and empathetic discussions with their maturing guardians about their necessities, inclinations, and wants. By cultivating open correspondence, the aide guarantees that kids can satisfy their obligations with straightforwardness, sympathy, and a promise to understanding the developing requirements of their folks.

The investigation reaches out to the possible effect of social, cultural, and familial assumptions on unambiguous providing care obligations. The aide urges youngsters to ponder their qualities, convictions, and the exceptional elements of their family, perceiving that providing care is a profoundly private excursion molded by individual conditions and social settings. By tending to these impacts, the aide engages kids to move toward their particular obligations with a feeling of legitimacy, social responsiveness, and a promise to regarding their family's remarkable elements.

A huge part of distinguishing explicit obligations is perceiving the developing idea of providing care jobs as guardians age. The aide recognizes that kids might have to adjust and alter their obligations in view of the changing requirements and conditions of their folks. By cultivating adaptability and flexibility, the aide guarantees that youngsters can explore the powerful idea of providing care with versatility and a promise to supporting the prosperity of their folks.

The investigation of explicit obligations consolidates the idea of guardian correspondence. The aide imparts that the consideration and support youngsters give to their maturing guardians are obligations as well as an equal trade of affection, regard, and appreciation. By outlining explicit obligations as a cooperative undertaking, the aide encourages a feeling of shared liability and solidarity inside the nuclear family.

The aide likewise addresses the potential difficulties related with kin elements in unambiguous providing care obligations. Kin might have changing viewpoints, obligations, and ways to deal with providing care. By recognizing the intricacies of kin connections, the aide gives direction on cultivating cooperation, settling clashes, and guaranteeing that particular providing care obligations are shared impartially.

Urgent to the investigation of explicit obligations is the acknowledgment of the recurrent idea of care inside the family. The aide accentuates that kids, when beneficiaries of care, presently have the chance to respond that consideration to their maturing guardians. By outlining explicit obligations as a characteristic expansion of the affection and backing got in before phases of life, the aide imparts in kids a feeling of obligation that is established in appreciation, regard, and a promise to saving the familial securities that interface ages.

The aide likewise investigates the possible effect of cultural assumptions and generalizations on kids' view of their particular providing care obligations. It urges youngsters to challenge generalizations, embrace the variety of providing care jobs, and perceive the novel qualities and commitments they bring to the providing care dynamic. By tending to cultural impacts, the aide enables youngsters to move toward their particular obligations with validness, strength, and a guarantee to reclassifying providing care inside the setting of their family's qualities.

Also, the aide underscores the idea of correspondence inside the family. It imparts that the consideration and support youngsters give to their maturing guardians are obligations as well as a complementary trade of affection, regard, and appreciation. By outlining explicit obligations as a cooperative undertaking, the aide cultivates a feeling of shared liability and solidarity inside the nuclear family.

The investigation of explicit obligations integrates the possibility of heritage inside the providing care venture. The aide perceives that the consideration gave to maturing guardians turns out to be essential for the family heritage — a demonstration of the persevering through bonds and values went down through ages. By recognizing the tradition of care, the aide motivates youngsters to move toward their particular obligations with a deep satisfaction, appreciation, and a promise to saving the familial tradition of adoration and backing.

Fundamentally, the part on distinguishing explicit obligations is a useful guidepost inside the more extensive providing care venture. By tending to substantial obligations, close to home intricacies, and the more extensive cultural effects on unambiguous providing care obligations, the aide furnishes kids with the information and outlook expected to offer help with credibility, empathy, and a profound obligation to protecting the prosperity and respect of their maturing guardians. This investigation highlights the all encompassing nature of providing care, underscoring that particular obligations are errands as well as significant articulations of adoration and correspondence inside the family.

### 3.2 Discussing the emotional and physical needs of aging parents

Inside the sympathetic aide, "Together Through Time: A Youngsters' Manual for Loving Maturing Guardians," the part diving into the "Profound and Actual Necessities of Maturing Guardians" unfurls as an empathetic investigation. This section is a piercing excursion, disclosing the nuanced scene of the close to home and actual necessities that request consideration and understanding as guardians navigate the later phases of life. By perceiving these necessities, kids are furnished with the information and awareness fundamental for offering significant help to their maturing guardians.

The investigation of feelings starts with a comprehension of the developing elements of parent-kid connections. The aide stresses that as guardians age, there is a characteristic change in close to home requirements that requires a sensitive and compassionate methodology. Kids are urged to perceive the profound scene of their maturing guardians, recognizing possible sensations of sentimentality, reflection, and the perplexing feelings related with the maturing system.

Also, the aide tends to the significance of friendship and basic encouragement. It perceives that maturing guardians might encounter sensations of forlornness or disconnection, particularly assuming they face actual constraints or changes in their groups of friends. By empowering kids to offer friendship, take part in significant discussions, and give a steady presence, the aide encourages a climate that tends to the feelings of maturing guardians with warmth and understanding.

The investigation stretches out to the expected effect of life advances on the profound prosperity of maturing guardians. The aide recognizes that critical life altering situations, like retirement or the passing of a companion, can achieve personal difficulties. Kids are encouraged to move toward these advances with awareness, perceiving the close to home effect they might have on their folks. By tending to these feelings, the aide guarantees that youngsters can offer help that supports the psychological and close to home versatility of their maturing guardians.

Urgent to the conversation of feelings is the investigation of correspondence. The aide stresses that transparent correspondence is a foundation of tending to the feelings of maturing guardians. Kids are urged to establish a climate where guardians feel happy with communicating their sentiments, wants, and concerns. By encouraging compelling correspondence, the aide guarantees that youngsters can explore the close to home intricacies of providing care with sympathy and a pledge to figuring out the remarkable feelings of their folks.

Besides, the investigation stretches out to the possible effect of social, cultural, and familial assumptions on the feelings of maturing guardians. The aide urges youngsters to consider their qualities, convictions, and the one of a kind elements of their family, perceiving that feelings are profoundly impacted by individual conditions and social settings. By tending to these impacts, the aide engages kids to move toward the feelings of their folks with social responsiveness, validness, and a guarantee to regarding their family's novel elements.

A huge part of tending to profound requirements is the acknowledgment of the different close to home scene of maturing guardians. The aide urges youngsters to tailor their methodology in light of the one of a kind feelings, inclinations, and social contemplations of their folks. By recognizing the independence of feelings, the aide guarantees that youngsters can offer close to home help that is delicate, customized, and aware.

The investigation of feelings likewise consolidates the idea of heritage inside the providing care venture. The aide perceives that basic encouragement turns out to be important for the family heritage — a demonstration of the persevering through bonds and values went down through ages. By recognizing the tradition of everyday reassurance, the aide rouses kids to move toward their jobs with a feeling of satisfaction, appreciation, and a pledge to saving the familial tradition of affection and understanding.

The investigation of actual requirements inside the part starts with an affirmation of the potential difficulties that maturing guardians might confront. The aide perceives that actual necessities can differ broadly and may incorporate versatility issues, persistent ailments, or the effect old enough related changes in tangible discernment. By tending to these difficulties, the aide furnishes youngsters with the information to offer actual help that is customized to the particular requirements of their folks.

Besides, the aide dives into the significance of keeping a solid way of life for maturing guardians. It perceives that actual prosperity is firmly interwoven with elements like sustenance, exercise, and preventive medical services measures. Youngsters are urged to team up with their folks in advancing a solid way of life, guaranteeing that their actual necessities are met in a complete and proactive way.

The investigation reaches out to the expected effect of ecological contemplations on the actual prosperity of maturing guardians. The aide urges kids to establish a living climate that is protected, open, and helpful for the actual solace of their folks. By tending to natural contemplations, the aide guarantees that youngsters can offer actual help that advances the prosperity and nobility of their maturing guardians.

Urgent to the conversation of actual necessities is the investigation of medical services liabilities. The aide perceives that overseeing medical services needs, prescriptions, and clinical arrangements might become necessary parts of providing care obligations. By giving direction on medical care contemplations, the aide guarantees that kids can explore these obligations with straightforwardness, obligation, and a promise to getting the actual prosperity of their folks.

Moreover, the investigation reaches out to the possible effect of social, cultural, and familial assumptions on the actual necessities of maturing guardians. The aide urges kids to consider their qualities, convictions, and the remarkable elements of their family, perceiving that actual requirements are profoundly impacted by individual conditions and social settings. By tending to these impacts, the aide engages youngsters to move toward the actual necessities of their folks with social responsiveness, genuineness, and a pledge to regarding their family's interesting elements.

A huge part of tending to actual requirements is the acknowledgment of the different actual scene of maturing guardians. The aide urges kids to tailor their methodology in view of the one of a kind actual requirements, inclinations, and social contemplations of their folks. By recognizing the independence of actual requirements, the aide guarantees that kids can offer actual help that is delicate, customized, and deferential.

The investigation of actual necessities likewise consolidates the idea of inheritance inside the providing care venture. The aide perceives that actual help turns out to be essential for the family inheritance — a demonstration of the persevering through bonds and values went down through ages. By recognizing the tradition of actual help, the aide rouses youngsters to move toward their jobs with a feeling of satisfaction, appreciation, and a guarantee to safeguarding the familial tradition of care and prosperity.

Fundamentally, the part on examining the profound and actual requirements of maturing guardians fills in as an extensive manual for understanding and tending to the multi-layered parts of care. By exploring the profound intricacies with compassion, compelling correspondence, and social responsiveness, youngsters can offer significant close to home help to their maturing guardians. All the while, by tending to the assorted actual requirements with information, proactive medical services measures, and natural contemplations, kids can guarantee the actual prosperity and nobility of their folks. This investigation highlights the comprehensive idea of providing care, underscoring that the close to home and actual necessities are interconnected aspects that merit smart consideration and a pledge to supporting the prosperity of maturing guardians inside the familial embroidery.

3.3 Providing examples of small acts of kindness that make a significant difference

Inside the humane aide, "Together Through Time: A Kids' Manual for Valuing Maturing Guardians," the section on "Giving Instances of Little Thoughtful gestures" unfurls as an endearing investigation. This section is a demonstration of the groundbreaking force of apparently little motions that, when woven together, make an embroidery of care and backing for maturing guardians. By enlightening the meaning of these demonstrations, the aide enables kids to leave on an excursion of graciousness that has a significant effect in the existences of their maturing guardians.

The investigation starts with an accentuation on the force of presence. The aide features that essentially investing energy with maturing guardians, participating in shared exercises, or partaking in a sincere discussion can be a significant thoughtful gesture. By perceiving the worth of presence, kids are urged to wind around the texture of association and friendship, encouraging a feeling of warmth and profound prosperity for their folks.

Besides, the aide dives into the significance of undivided attention as a little thoughtful gesture. It perceives that maturing guardians might have stories, recollections, and insight to share. By effectively tuning in and showing certifiable interest in their folks' encounters, youngsters approve their folks' points of view as well as make snapshots of association and it are profoundly significant to figure out that.

The investigation stretches out to the meaning of offering thanks. The aide urges kids to convey their appreciation for hell's sake, direction, and penances their folks have made all through their lives. By offering thanks, kids add to a positive and certifying close to home climate, recognizing the significant effect their folks have had on shaping their lives.

Moreover, the aide underlines the benefit of integrating straightforward yet acts of kindness into everyday schedules. This can incorporate setting up a most loved dinner, bringing some tea, or astonishing guardians with a little gift. These motions, however apparently unobtrusive, convey a strong message of adoration, care, and thoughtfulness regarding the inclinations and necessities of maturing guardians.

The investigation of little thoughtful gestures likewise consolidates the idea of making a memory container or scrapbook. The aide recommends that youngsters can gather and report valued recollections, tokens, or notes that praise the extraordinary minutes imparted to their folks. By making a substantial portrayal of these recollections, youngsters add to a tradition of affection and association that can be returned to and treasured over the long run.

Vital to the conversation of little thoughtful gestures is the investigation of integrating humor and happiness into day to day collaborations. The aide perceives the helpful worth of chuckling and delight, particularly despite challenges. Kids are urged to share happy minutes, jokes, or take part in exercises that give a feeling of pleasure and levity into the existences of their maturing guardians.

The investigation reaches out to the likely effect of assertions and positive attesting words. The aide urges kids to offer uplifting statements, appreciation, and certification to their folks. By expressing adoration and backing, kids add to a positive profound climate, encouraging a feeling of safety and prosperity for their maturing guardians.

Besides, the aide digs into the idea of making a mitigating and encouraging climate. This can include playing quieting music, consolidating fragrant healing, or organizing a comfortable and tranquil space inside the home. By taking care of the tactile encounters of their folks, youngsters establish a climate that advances unwinding, solace, and close to home prosperity.

The investigation of little thoughtful gestures consolidates the idea of helping with everyday exercises. While apparently standard, assisting with undertakings, for example, shopping for food, sorting out family tasks, or getting things done can be significantly significant for maturing guardians. By offering functional help, kids add to the simplicity and solace of their folks' day to day routines.

Furthermore, the aide perceives the significance of praising achievements, both of all shapes and sizes. Kids are urged to recognize and remember critical minutes, accomplishments, or even normal triumphs in the existences of their maturing guardians. By praising achievements, youngsters make a culture of appreciation and affirmation, confirming the worth of their folks' process.

Significant to the conversation of little thoughtful gestures is the investigation of integrating innovation to connect distances. The aide perceives that in the present interconnected world, kids can utilize innovation to remain associated with their maturing guardians, whether through video calls, sharing photographs, or partaking in virtual exercises together. By utilizing innovation, kids defeat actual distances and keep a feeling of closeness and association.

The investigation stretches out to the expected effect of including maturing guardians in navigation. The aide urges kids to look for their folks' contribution on issues that influence their lives. By including guardians in direction, youngsters convey a feeling of regard, independence, and organization, certifying the proceeded with significance of their folks' viewpoints and inclinations.

Besides, the aide stresses the benefit of establishing a steady and comprehensive social climate for maturing guardians. This can include working with social communications, associating with local area assets, or orchestrating get-togethers with loved ones. By cultivating social associations, youngsters add to the close to home prosperity and feeling of having a place for their maturing guardians.

The investigation of little thoughtful gestures integrates the idea of encouraging an affection for deep rooted learning. The aide recommends that youngsters can draw in their folks in exercises that animate the psyche, like perusing together, investigating new leisure activities, or partaking in instructive projects. By cultivating an adoration for learning, youngsters add to the mental prosperity and feeling of satisfaction for their maturing guardians.

Besides, the aide digs into the meaning of keeping a positive and hopeful standpoint. Youngsters are urged to move toward difficulties with flexibility, showing an inspirational perspective that can rouse and elevate their maturing guardians. By typifying a feeling of confidence, youngsters add to a confident and steady profound climate.

The investigation stretches out to the possible effect of making an inheritance project together. The aide proposes that kids and their folks can team up on a venture that mirrors their common qualities, recollections, or goals. By taking part in a heritage project, youngsters add to an unmistakable portrayal of the persevering through connection between ages, making a significant and enduring recognition.

Urgent to the conversation of little thoughtful gestures is the investigation of integrating care and unwinding strategies. The aide perceives the likely advantages of practices like contemplation, profound breathing, or delicate practices in advancing close to home and actual prosperity. By integrating care, youngsters add to a feeling of quiet, serenity, and by and large health for their maturing guardians.

Also, the aide digs into the idea of offering consolation and solace during testing minutes. Maturing guardians might confront vulnerabilities, fears, or snapshots of weakness. Kids are urged to give consolation, an encouraging presence, and a feeling that all is well with the world during such occasions. By offering daily encouragement, youngsters add to a feeling of safety and prosperity for their folks.

The investigation of little thoughtful gestures consolidates the idea of commending and regarding family customs. The aide recommends that kids can proceed or lay out customs that hold wistful incentive for their maturing guardians. By commending family customs, kids add to a feeling of coherence, association, and delight inside the familial embroidery.

Moreover, the aide accentuates the benefit of supporting profound prosperity. This can include taking part in shared profound works on, partaking in strict or social services, or basically making a space for reflection and examination. By taking care of the otherworldly requirements of their folks, kids add to a feeling of inward harmony, reason, and connectedness.

The investigation stretches out to the expected effect of making a steady providing care organization. The aide perceives that providing care is a common obligation, and kids can team up with kin, more distant family, or local area assets to offer far reaching help for their maturing guardians. By cultivating a providing care organization, youngsters guarantee that their folks get comprehensive consideration that tends to both profound and actual requirements.

Critical to the conversation of little thoughtful gestures is the investigation of integrating innovativeness and creative articulation. The aide urges kids to participate in imaginative exercises, like workmanship, music, or narrating, with their maturing guardians. By cultivating imaginative articulation, kids add to a feeling of delight, self-articulation, and shared snapshots of creative investigation.

Also, the aide digs into the idea of advancing taking care of oneself for maturing guardians. Youngsters are urged to help their folks in keeping a good arrangement between providing care liabilities and individual prosperity. By advancing taking care of oneself, youngsters add to the general wellbeing, flexibility, and essentialness of their maturing guardians.

The investigation of little thoughtful gestures integrates the idea of making a customized care plan. The aide recommends that youngsters can work cooperatively with their folks to foster a consideration plan that lines up with their exceptional necessities, inclinations, and desires. By fitting consideration to individual conditions, kids add to a providing care approach that is delicate, customized, and deferential.

Besides, the aide underscores the benefit of taking part in memory and narrating. Youngsters are urged to set out open doors for their folks to share stories, think back about critical minutes, and pass down astuteness. By participating in narrating, youngsters add to a feeling of congruity, association, and the safeguarding of family stories.

The investigation stretches out to the likely effect of pushing for maturing guardians inside medical services settings. The aide perceives that kids might have to explore medical services frameworks, speak with clinical experts, and guarantee that their folks get extensive and empathetic consideration. By pushing for medical services needs, youngsters add to the actual prosperity and pride of their maturing guardians.

Pivotal to the conversation of little thoughtful gestures is the investigation of consolidating intergenerational exercises. The aide urges youngsters to set out open doors for associations between various ages, whether through family get-togethers, local area occasions, or joint exercises. By cultivating intergenerational associations, kids add to a feeling of local area, shared encounters, and common help.

Besides, the aide digs into the idea of giving consolation and solace during seasons of change. Maturing guardians might encounter changes in living game plans, medical issue, or everyday schedules. Kids are urged to offer consolation, direction, and a feeling of strength during these changes. By offering help during seasons of progress, kids add to a smooth and genuinely steady providing care venture.

The investigation stretches out to the likely effect of integrating innovation to upgrade correspondence and association. The aide perceives that kids can utilize innovation to work with correspondence, share updates, and remain associated with their maturing guardians, particularly on the off chance that actual distances represent a test. By utilizing innovation, kids add to a feeling of closeness and commitment.

Vital to the conversation of little thoughtful gestures is the investigation of the likely effect of recognizing and tending to inner difficulties. The aide perceives that maturing guardians might encounter a scope of feelings, including sorrow, dread, or vulnerability. Kids are urged to move toward these personal difficulties with compassion, responsiveness, and a guarantee to offering close to home help. By recognizing and tending to profound necessities, kids add to the general prosperity and flexibility of their maturing guardians.

# Chapter 4

Effective Communication

In the complex embroidery of providing care investigated inside "Together Through Time: A Youngsters' Manual for Valuing Maturing Guardians," the section on "Successful Correspondence" arises as a crucial foundation. This section enlightens the significant effect of clear, compassionate, and open correspondence in exploring the intricacies of the maturing system. By digging into the subtleties of viable correspondence, the aide outfits youngsters with the devices expected to encourage understanding, reinforce associations, and explore the advancing elements intrinsic in focusing on maturing guardians.

The investigation starts with an acknowledgment of the developing idea of parent-youngster connections as guardians age. The aide accentuates the significance of adjusting correspondence styles to oblige the changing necessities and elements of the relationship. By perceiving that correspondence is a powerful interaction, kids are engaged to move toward discussions with adaptability, receptiveness, and a guarantee to grasping the exceptional points of view of their maturing guardians.

Besides, the aide highlights the meaning of undivided attention as a fundamental component of viable correspondence. It urges kids to be completely present, drew in, and mindful while speaking with their maturing guardians. By rehearsing undivided attention, youngsters establish a climate that encourages shared figuring out, approval, and the development of more profound associations.

The investigation stretches out to the possible effect of non-verbal correspondence signals. The aide perceives that non-verbal communication, looks, and motions assume a critical part in passing on messages and feelings. Youngsters are urged to be aware of these non-verbal signs, encouraging a mindfulness that improves the extravagance and profundity of correspondence with their maturing guardians.

Moreover, the aide digs into the significance of persistence and sympathy in viable correspondence. It recognizes that maturing guardians might confront difficulties in putting themselves out there or articulating their requirements. By moving toward discussions with persistence and sympathy, youngsters make a strong space that urges their folks to convey all the more transparently and serenely.

The investigation of viable correspondence integrates the idea of making a safe and non-critical space for exchange. The aide recommends that kids can lay out a climate where guardians feel open to offering their viewpoints, concerns, and feelings unafraid of judgment. By cultivating a non-critical space, kids work with transparent correspondence that fortifies the bonds inside the family.

Urgent to the conversation of viable correspondence is the investigation of approving and recognizing guardians' viewpoints. The aide underscores that recognizing the contemplations, sentiments, and encounters of maturing guardians adds to a feeling of regard and understanding. By approving their points of view, youngsters insist the worth of their folks' lived encounters and encourage a more profound association based on common regard.

Additionally, the aide digs into the possible effect of social, cultural, and familial assumptions on correspondence elements. It urges youngsters to consider their qualities, convictions, and the special elements of their family, perceiving that successful correspondence is impacted by individual conditions and social settings. By tending to these impacts, the aide enables youngsters to move toward correspondence with social responsiveness, genuineness, and a promise to respecting their family's exceptional elements.

A huge part of compelling correspondence is the investigation of starting discussions about significant subjects. The aide perceives that specific subjects, for example, medical care inclinations, end-of-life arranging, or monetary issues, might be delicate however critical to address.

Youngsters are urged to move toward these discussions with responsiveness, transparency, and a guarantee to figuring out their folks' desires. By starting these conversations, kids add to a proactive and informed providing care approach that lines up with their folks' qualities.

The investigation reaches out to the expected effect of shared dynamic in the providing care dynamic. The aide perceives that youngsters might have to team up with their maturing guardians in pursuing choices connected with medical services, living courses of action, or different parts of their lives. By including guardians in navigation, youngsters confirm their office, inclinations, and independence, cultivating a cooperative methodology that esteems their folks' feedback.

Besides, the aide underlines the significance of adjusting correspondence procedures to oblige changes in mental capacities. It recognizes that maturing guardians might encounter mental degradation, affecting their correspondence capacities. Kids are urged to adjust their correspondence styles, utilize clear and basic language, and utilize persistence while taking part in discussions with guardians confronting mental difficulties.

The investigation of viable correspondence consolidates the idea of using innovation to improve association. The aide perceives that innovation can be a significant device for keeping up with correspondence, particularly in situations where actual distances represent a test. By utilizing innovation, youngsters can remain associated with their maturing guardians through video calls, informing, and other computerized stages, cultivating a feeling of closeness and commitment.

Pivotal to the conversation of compelling correspondence is the investigation of tending to likely struggles or conflicts. The aide perceives that distinctions in points of view might emerge, and clashes are a characteristic piece of any relationship. Kids are urged to move toward clashes with sympathy, undivided attention, and a pledge to tracking down commonly pleasing arrangements. By exploring clashes with deference, kids add to a correspondence climate that encourages understanding and goal.

Besides, the aide dives into the idea of offering close to home help through correspondence. It recognizes that maturing guardians might encounter a scope of feelings, including distress, dread, or vulnerability. Kids are urged to offer a listening ear, uplifting statements, and consolation during sincerely testing times. By offering close to home help through correspondence, kids add to the general prosperity and strength of their maturing guardians.

The investigation reaches out to the likely effect of integrating humor and delight into correspondence. The aide perceives the restorative worth of giggling and euphoria, particularly even with difficulties.

Youngsters are urged to share carefree minutes, jokes, or take part in exercises that give a feeling of pleasure and levity into their discussions with maturing guardians. By integrating humor, youngsters add to a positive and elevating correspondence dynamic.

Urgent to the conversation of powerful correspondence is the investigation of cultivating a feeling of consideration and interest. The aide perceives that maturing guardians might have important experiences, stories, and insight to share. Youngsters are urged to set out open doors for their folks to partake in discussions, share their encounters, and add to family conversations. By cultivating incorporation, kids confirm the significance of their folks' viewpoints inside the family story.

The investigation of compelling correspondence consolidates the idea of giving updates and remaining associated. The aide proposes that youngsters can keep their maturing guardians informed about family news, occasions, and exercises. By giving customary updates, youngsters make a feeling of association and contribution, keeping their folks participated in the unfurling sections of day to day life.

Moreover, the aide digs into the significance of offering thanks and appreciation through correspondence. It recognizes the effect of asserting words, articulations of appreciation, and affirmation of the commitments made by maturing guardians. Kids are urged to convey their appreciation for hell's sake, direction, and penances their folks have made all through their lives. By offering thanks, kids add to a positive and confirming correspondence climate.

The investigation stretches out to the possible effect of shared narrating and memory. The aide perceives that narrating gives a strong road to association and understanding. Kids are urged to set out open doors for their folks to share stories, think back about critical minutes, and pass down astuteness. By participating in shared narrating, kids add to the conservation of family stories and make snapshots of association that range ages.

Urgent to the conversation of powerful correspondence is the investigation of overseeing assumptions and being reasonable about correspondence abilities. The aide perceives that maturing might get changes hearing, vision, or mental capacities, influencing correspondence. Youngsters are urged to show restraint, versatile, and sensible in their assumptions, adjusting correspondence methodologies to oblige the developing necessities of their folks.

Besides, the aide dives into the idea of tending to language obstructions or contrasts. In multicultural or multilingual families, youngsters might have to explore correspondence challenges emerging from language contrasts. The aide urges kids to track down comprehensive and available ways of imparting, guaranteeing that language obstructions don't prevent understanding or association.

The investigation of compelling correspondence integrates the idea of integrating customs or schedules into day to day connections. The aide recommends that kids can lay out schedules, like standard registrations, shared exercises, or assigned times for discussions, making an anticipated and encouraging correspondence dynamic. By integrating ceremonies, youngsters add to a feeling of congruity and association inside the providing care relationship.

Moreover, the aide accentuates the significance of regarding security and limits in correspondence. It recognizes that maturing guardians, similar to anybody, may have inclinations for the degree of protection they want. Youngsters are urged to be aware of these limits, regarding their folks' requirement for individual space and independence in correspondence.

The investigation reaches out to the expected effect of adjusting correspondence methodologies to oblige tactile changes. The aide perceives that maturing might get changes tangible insight, like hearing or vision misfortune. Youngsters are urged to adjust their correspondence styles, utilizing clear and open language, guaranteeing appropriate lighting, and utilizing methodologies that upgrade correspondence for guardians encountering tactile changes.

Essential to the conversation of powerful correspondence is the investigation of the expected effect of innovation in connecting correspondence holes. The aide perceives that innovation can be an important device for upgrading correspondence, particularly in situations where actual distances represent a test. Youngsters can investigate the utilization of video calls, informing applications, or other computerized stages to remain associated with their maturing guardians, cultivating a feeling of closeness and commitment.

Also, the aide digs into the idea of sustaining intergenerational correspondence. It perceives the wealth that comes from associations between various ages inside the family. Youngsters are urged to set out open doors for intergenerational correspondence, whether through family social events, joint exercises, or shared encounters. By encouraging intergenerational associations, kids add to a feeling of local area, shared values, and common getting it.

The investigation of powerful correspondence integrates the idea of using inventive and elective specialized strategies. The aide recommends that kids can investigate imaginative roads like workmanship, music, or signals to speak with their maturing guardians. By embracing elective techniques, kids can beat potential correspondence obstructions and make significant associations.

Besides, the aide underscores the benefit of participating in joint exercises as a type of correspondence. Shared exercises, whether side interests, games, or trips, can act as a strong method for correspondence. Kids are urged to investigate exercises that line up with their folks' advantages, making snapshots of association that rise above verbal correspondence.

The investigation reaches out to the likely effect of integrating care and presence into correspondence. The aide perceives the benefit of being completely present and mindful during discussions. Youngsters are urged to rehearse care, zeroing in on the current second, and moving toward correspondence with a feeling of quiet and mindfulness. By integrating care, kids establish a climate that encourages significant and centered correspondence.

Vital to the conversation of successful correspondence is the investigation of the possible effect of social capability. The aide perceives that viable correspondence is impacted by social settings, convictions, and practices. Kids are urged to be socially capable, taking into account the different foundations and viewpoints that might shape correspondence elements. By embracing social responsiveness, youngsters guarantee that correspondence is deferential, comprehensive, and obliging of their folks' social impacts.

Also, the aide digs into the idea of adjusting correspondence techniques to oblige exceptional relational peculiarities. Each family has its own elements, molded by variables like size, design, and connections. Kids are urged to be versatile in their correspondence draws near, perceiving the subtleties of their family's extraordinary elements and fitting correspondence techniques likewise.

The investigation of viable correspondence integrates the idea of making a tradition of correspondence. The aide recommends that kids can take part in discussions that add to the conservation of family stories, values, and shrewdness. By encouraging a tradition of correspondence, kids guarantee that the rich embroidery of their family's story is gone down through ages, making a significant and persevering through association.

4.1 Teaching children the importance of open and honest communication

Inside the clever aide, "Together Through Time: A Kids' Manual for Valuing Maturing Guardians," the section on "Showing Youngsters the Significance of Transparent Correspondence" unfurls as an essential establishment. This portion dives into the meaning of imparting in kids the upsides of straightforwardness, sympathy, and powerful correspondence as they explore the mind boggling excursion of really focusing on their maturing guardians. By investigating the subtleties of transparent correspondence, the aide furnishes youngsters with the devices to encourage understanding, form trust, and develop significant associations with their folks as they age.

The investigation starts by featuring the extraordinary force of open correspondence inside the parent-youngster relationship. The aide underscores that cultivating a culture of receptiveness lays the basis for shared understanding and trust. By training youngsters to convey transparently, guardians furnish them with the abilities to explore the advancing elements that accompany the maturing system.

Besides, the aide highlights the significance of trustworthiness as a core value in correspondence. Youngsters are urged to embrace genuineness as a foundation of their connections with maturing guardians. This includes being honest about their own sentiments, concerns, and encounters while establishing a climate that urges guardians to genuinely put themselves out there.

The investigation reaches out to the likely effect of making a safe and non-critical space for open correspondence. The aide recommends that kids can lay out a climate where guardians feel open to offering their viewpoints, concerns, and feelings unafraid of judgment. By cultivating a non-critical space, kids guarantee that their folks can convey straightforwardly, making an establishment for trust and understanding.

Urgent to the conversation of transparent correspondence is the investigation of undivided attention. The aide underscores that powerful correspondence is a two-way road, expecting kids to pay attention to their maturing guardians effectively. By leveling up their listening abilities, youngsters exhibit compassion and make a space for guardians to straightforwardly share their considerations and encounters.

Also, the aide dives into the idea of recognizing and approving guardians' points of view. It stresses that open correspondence includes perceiving the legitimacy of guardians' sentiments, encounters, and perspectives. Youngsters are urged to communicate compassion, insist the significance of their folks' points of view, and approve their feelings, encouraging a more profound degree of understanding.

The investigation of transparent correspondence consolidates the idea of starting discussions about significant points. The aide perceives that specific subjects, for example, medical services inclinations, end-of-life arranging, or monetary issues, might be delicate however vital to address. Kids are encouraged to move toward these discussions with responsiveness, transparency, and a pledge to grasping their folks' desires.

Urgent to the conversation is the investigation of the possible effect of shared direction. The aide perceives that kids might have to team up with their maturing guardians in settling on choices connected with medical care, living game plans, or different parts of their lives. By including guardians in navigation, youngsters certify their organization, inclinations, and independence, cultivating a cooperative methodology that esteems their folks' feedback.

Besides, the aide underlines the significance of adjusting correspondence systems to oblige changes in mental capacities. It recognizes that maturing guardians might encounter mental degradation, influencing their correspondence capacities. Kids are urged to adjust their correspondence styles, utilize clear and straightforward language, and utilize persistence while participating in discussions with guardians confronting mental difficulties.

The investigation of showing youngsters the significance of transparent correspondence integrates the idea of making customs or schedules that work with exchange. The aide proposes that kids can lay out schedules, like normal registrations, shared exercises, or assigned times for discussions, making an anticipated and encouraging correspondence dynamic. By consolidating ceremonies, youngsters add to a feeling of progression and association inside the providing care relationship.

Besides, the aide digs into the idea of using innovation to upgrade correspondence. It perceives that innovation can be an important device for keeping up with correspondence, particularly in situations where actual distances represent a test. Youngsters can investigate the utilization of video calls, informing applications, or other computerized stages to remain associated with their maturing guardians, cultivating a feeling of closeness and commitment.

The investigation stretches out to the possible effect of consolidating imaginative and elective specialized strategies. The aide proposes that kids can investigate inventive roads like craftsmanship, music, or motions to speak with their maturing guardians. By embracing elective strategies, kids can beat potential correspondence boundaries and make significant associations.

Pivotal to the conversation is the investigation of overseeing assumptions and being reasonable about correspondence capacities. The aide perceives that maturing might get changes hearing, vision, or mental capacities, influencing correspondence. Youngsters are urged to show restraint, versatile, and practical in their assumptions, adjusting correspondence systems to oblige the advancing necessities of their folks.

In addition, the aide digs into the idea of tending to language obstructions or contrasts. In multicultural or multilingual families, youngsters might have to explore correspondence challenges emerging from language contrasts. The aide urges kids to track down comprehensive and available ways of imparting, guaranteeing that language boundaries don't prevent understanding or association.

The investigation of showing youngsters the significance of transparent correspondence integrates the idea of sustaining intergenerational correspondence. The aide proposes that kids can set out open doors for intergenerational correspondence, whether through family get-togethers, joint exercises, or shared encounters. By encouraging intergenerational associations, kids add to a feeling of local area, shared values, and common getting it.

Besides, the aide underscores the benefit of participating in joint exercises as a type of correspondence. Shared exercises, whether side interests, games, or trips, can act as a strong method for correspondence. Kids are urged to investigate exercises that line up with their folks' advantages, making snapshots of association that rise above verbal correspondence.

The investigation stretches out to the likely effect of integrating care and presence into correspondence. The aide perceives the benefit of being completely present and mindful during discussions. Youngsters are urged to rehearse care, zeroing in on the current second, and moving toward correspondence with a feeling of quiet and mindfulness. By consolidating care, youngsters establish a climate that cultivates significant and centered correspondence.

Vital to the conversation is the investigation of the likely effect of social skill. The aide perceives that powerful correspondence is affected by social settings, convictions, and practices. Youngsters are urged to be socially equipped, taking into account the different foundations and viewpoints that might shape correspondence elements. By embracing social awareness, youngsters guarantee that correspondence is deferential, comprehensive, and obliging of their folks' social impacts.

The investigation of showing kids the significance of transparent correspondence consolidates the idea of adjusting correspondence techniques to oblige interesting relational peculiarities. Each family has its own elements, molded by variables like size, design, and connections. Youngsters are urged to be versatile in their correspondence draws near, perceiving the subtleties of their family's exceptional elements and fitting correspondence systems appropriately.

Besides, the aide dives into the idea of making a tradition of correspondence. It recommends that kids can participate in discussions that add to the safeguarding of family stories, values, and astuteness. By encouraging a tradition of correspondence, kids guarantee that the rich embroidery of their family's story is gone down through ages, making a significant and persevering through association.

4.2 Providing age-appropriate communication strategies

Inside the empathetic aide, "Together Through Time: A Kids' Manual for Treasuring Maturing Guardians," the part on "Giving Age-Suitable Correspondence Systems" unfurls as a significant compass. This section dives into the nuanced specialty of fitting correspondence for youngsters, guaranteeing that the exchange encompassing the maturing system isn't just available yet additionally significant. By investigating age-proper correspondence procedures, the aide furnishes guardians with the devices to encourage understanding, mitigate concerns, and sustain a strong climate as they explore the mind boggling excursion of really focusing on their maturing guardians.

The investigation starts with an acknowledgment of the different formative phases of life as a youngster. The aide highlights the significance of adjusting correspondence techniques to line up with the mental and profound limits of youngsters at various ages. By recognizing these distinctions, guardians can tailor their methodology, guaranteeing that the data shared isn't just intelligible yet in addition logically pertinent to the kid's transformative phase.

Also, the aide dives into the idea of starting open discussions since the beginning. It underscores the benefit of laying out an underpinning of correspondence that urges youngsters to offer their viewpoints, sentiments, and questions. By cultivating a climate where exchange is invited, guardians make a space where youngsters feel open to looking for understanding and sharing their own viewpoints.

The investigation stretches out to the likely effect of utilizing age-proper language. The aide perceives that the decision of language assumes a critical part in viable correspondence with youngsters. Guardians are urged to utilize language that is clear, basic, and customized to the kid's age and understanding level. By choosing age-fitting words and clarifications, guardians guarantee that the data is open and significant for their youngsters.

Critical to the conversation old enough suitable correspondence techniques is the investigation of using narrating and accounts. The aide recommends that guardians can pass complex ideas about maturing on through age-suitable stories, tales, or accounts. By outlining the data inside a narrating setting, guardians draw in the kid's creative mind, making the topic more engaging and edible.

In addition, the aide dives into the idea of resolving youngsters' inquiries with trustworthiness and effortlessness. It underscores the significance of answering youngsters' requests in an honest yet age-proper way.

Guardians are urged to give clear and succinct responses, keeping away from pointless subtleties that might overpower or confound the youngster. By resolving inquiries with genuineness and effortlessness, guardians make an underpinning of trust and straightforwardness.

The investigation old enough suitable correspondence techniques integrates the idea of utilizing visual guides. The aide recommends that visual portrayals, like outlines, drawings, or age-fitting books, can upgrade's comprehension kids might interpret complex subjects connected with maturing. By integrating visual guides, guardians take care of various learning styles and give extra layers of perception.

Critical to the conversation is the investigation of normalizing the maturing system through age-suitable models. The aide perceives that youngsters might better comprehend the idea of maturing through engaging models inside their own family or through age-suitable stories. Guardians are urged to feature positive parts of the maturing system, for example, acquiring intelligence or encountering new experiences, to encourage a positive and standardized perspective on maturing.

Also, the aide dives into the expected effect of utilizing representations or relationships. Guardians can utilize age-proper allegories or similarities to make sense of complicated parts of maturing in wording that youngsters can get a handle on more without any problem. By attracting equals to recognizable ideas, guardians work with a more profound comprehension of the maturing system and its importance.

The investigation old enough proper correspondence systems integrates the idea of tending to feelings and sentiments. The aide perceives that conversations about maturing might bring out different feelings in youngsters. Guardians are urged to recognize and approve these feelings, making a space for kids to communicate their sentiments and concerns. By tending to feelings, guardians sustain a strong climate that recognizes the youngster's personal prosperity.

Besides, the aide underlines the significance of consolidating play and intelligent exercises. Guardians can utilize age-fitting games, pretending, or intelligent exercises to draw in kids in discussions about maturing. By making the growing experience intuitive and charming, guardians make positive relationship with the subject and energize dynamic cooperation from their youngsters.

The investigation stretches out to the likely effect of including kids in providing care exercises. Contingent upon their age and capacities, youngsters can be remembered for age-suitable providing care errands, for example, helping with basic tasks or investing quality energy with their maturing grandparents. By including kids in providing care, guardians encourage a feeling of obligation, compassion, and association with the maturing system.

Critical to the conversation old enough proper correspondence methodologies is the investigation of raising a steady climate for doubts and investigation. The aide highlights the significance of developing a climate where kids feel open to getting clarification on some pressing issues and investigating their interest in maturing. Guardians are urged to be open, patient, and receptive to their youngsters' requests, making a dynamic where correspondence is a nonstop and developing cycle.

Additionally, the aide digs into the idea of encouraging age-proper autonomy. Contingent upon the kid's age, guardians can energize a level of freedom in understanding and partaking in conversations about maturing. This might include permitting more seasoned youngsters to explore specific angles freely or empowering them to offer their viewpoints and viewpoints. By cultivating autonomy, guardians engage youngsters to play a functioning job in their comprehension own might interpret the maturing system.

The investigation old enough fitting correspondence methodologies integrates the idea of consolidating innovation and age-proper media. The aide proposes that guardians can utilize age-proper recordings, applications, or online assets to enhance conversations about maturing. By utilizing innovation, guardians give extra channels to kids to investigate and comprehend the point in an organization that reverberates with their age.

Pivotal to the conversation is the investigation of tending to likely feelings of trepidation or misinterpretations. The aide perceives that kids might foster feelings of trepidation or confusions about maturing. Guardians are urged to address these worries with persistence and sympathy, scattering legends and giving age-proper consolation. By recognizing and tending to fears, guardians make a groundwork of understanding that eases youngsters' nerves.

Besides, the aide digs into the likely effect of consolidating age-fitting good examples. Youngsters might profit from positive good examples who epitomize the maturing system in a solid and dynamic manner. Guardians can present age-fitting stories, histories, or instances of people who have embraced maturing with elegance, flexibility, and an uplifting perspective. By giving positive good examples, guardians shape a story that stresses the potential for a satisfying and significant life at each stage.

The investigation old enough fitting correspondence procedures integrates the idea of setting out open doors for reflection and articulation. Guardians can urge youngsters to offer their viewpoints, sentiments, and points of view through age-suitable innovative outlets like craftsmanship, composing, or conversations. By giving outlets to articulation, guardians cultivate a feeling of independence and self-appearance in their kids.

Besides, the aide underlines the significance of returning to and supporting age-suitable data. Understanding and points of view advance as youngsters develop, and guardians are urged to occasionally return to conversations about maturing. This permits guardians to fit data to the youngster's rising mental capacities and address new different kinds of feedback that might emerge as they mature.

The investigation reaches out to the possible effect of including kids in intergenerational exercises. Guardians can set out open doors for kids to take part in intergenerational exercises, whether through family social occasions, local area occasions, or joint ventures. By encouraging intergenerational associations, guardians furnish youngsters with firsthand encounters that add to a more profound comprehension of the maturing system.

Significant to the conversation old enough fitting correspondence techniques is the investigation of tending to the different requirements and characters of kin. The aide perceives that kin inside a family might have various requirements, viewpoints, and responses to conversations about maturing. Guardians are urged to tailor correspondence systems to oblige the exceptional qualities of every youngster, guaranteeing that data is conveyed in a way that resounds with their singular inclinations and understanding.

Besides, the aide digs into the idea of developing a family culture that values open correspondence. Guardians can effectively mold a family culture that focuses on open discourse, sympathy, and understanding. By cultivating an open climate, guardians make an enduring establishment that upholds youngsters in exploring the intricacies of the maturing system inside the family setting.

The investigation old enough proper correspondence techniques consolidates the idea of looking for proficient direction when required. In situations where youngsters might need extra help or have explicit worries, guardians are urged to look for direction from experts like kid analysts, advisors, or teachers. Proficient direction can offer fitted methodologies to address the exceptional requirements and conditions of every kid.

Urgent to the conversation is the investigation of the possible effect of integrating instructive assets and age-suitable books. The aide perceives the worth old enough proper writing in working with conversations about maturing. Guardians can utilize books and instructive assets that take special care of the youngster's age and cognizance level, giving data in an organization that is drawing in and engaging.

Besides, the aide dives into the idea of displaying positive correspondence ways of behaving. Guardians act as essential good examples for their kids, and by showing positive correspondence ways of behaving, they set a model for solid discourse. By demonstrating undivided attention, sympathy, and transparency, guardians add to a family culture that values viable correspondence.

The investigation old enough proper correspondence procedures integrates the idea of adjusting correspondence ways to deal with individual learning styles. Kids might have different learning styles, and guardians are urged to be adaptable in their methodology. By perceiving and adjusting to individual learning inclinations, guardians guarantee that data is conveyed in a manner that resounds with every youngster's exceptional approach to handling data.

Pivotal to the conversation is the investigation of the likely effect of making an input circle. The aide perceives the significance of making a continuous exchange where youngsters feel open to giving criticism on the correspondence cycle. Guardians can effectively look for input from their youngsters, changing correspondence procedures in view of their criticism and developing necessities. By making a criticism circle, guardians show a promise to ceaseless improvement in correspondence.

Besides, the aide dives into the idea of cultivating a feeling of shared liability in figuring out maturing. Guardians can stress that comprehension and exploring the maturing system is a common obligation inside the family. By cultivating a feeling of aggregate commitment, guardians urge kids to effectively take part in conversations, clarify pressing issues, and add to the family's common perspective of maturing.

The investigation old enough proper correspondence systems integrates the idea of being receptive to social and cultural impacts. The aide perceives that social and cultural variables might shape youngsters' points of view on maturing. Guardians are urged to be sensitive to these impacts, tending to social or cultural misguided judgments and giving data that adjusts the family's qualities and convictions.

4.3 Addressing common challenges in discussing sensitive topics with aging parents

Inside the caring aide, "Together Through Time: A Youngsters' Manual for Valuing Maturing Guardians," the part on "Tending to Normal Difficulties in Examining Delicate Points with Maturing Guardians" unfurls as a pivotal and sympathetic compass.

This portion dives into the multifaceted elements of exploring delicate discussions with maturing guardians, perceiving the difficulties that might emerge and giving reasonable techniques to encouraging open and significant exchange. By tending to these difficulties, the aide furnishes youngsters with the devices to move toward delicate subjects with sympathy, regard, and a profound comprehension of the intricacies inborn in the maturing system.

The investigation starts by recognizing the intrinsic awareness of specific subjects connected with maturing, for example, medical services choices, end-of-life arranging, or changes in living plans. The aide underscores that these discussions can inspire a scope of feelings and worries for the two youngsters and their maturing guardians. By perceiving the responsiveness of these subjects, kids are urged to move toward conversations with an uplifted consciousness of the profound subtleties included.

Besides, the aide dives into the likely test of exploring varying points of view and inclinations. Youngsters and their maturing guardians might have various perspectives on specific touchy points, and exploring these distinctions requires a sensitive and deferential methodology. The aide urges kids to look for understanding, listen effectively, and recognize the legitimacy of their folks' viewpoints, cultivating a climate where contrasting perspectives can coincide with compassion and regard.

The investigation stretches out to the test of conquering social or generational restrictions encompassing specific delicate subjects. Social or generational contrasts might impact the receptiveness with which maturing guardians approach specific subjects. The aide perceives the significance of social responsiveness and urges kids to move toward discussions with mindfulness and regard for their folks' social or generational points of view. By exploring these restrictions with care, youngsters make a space where conversations can unfurl with understanding and social capability.

Urgent to the conversation of tending to normal difficulties is the investigation of potential correspondence obstructions that might emerge. Maturing guardians might confront difficulties in putting themselves out there, whether because of mental deterioration, tangible changes, or different variables. Kids are urged to move toward discussions with persistence, versatility, and a guarantee to making a protected and steady space for their folks to really impart. By tending to correspondence boundaries, youngsters add to a more comprehensive and compassionate discourse.

In addition, the aide dives into the test of dealing with close to home responses that might emerge during delicate discussions. The two kids and maturing guardians might encounter a scope of feelings, including dread, bitterness, or vulnerability.

The aide underlines the significance of recognizing and approving these feelings, establishing a climate where the two players feel upheld in communicating their sentiments. By dealing with close to home responses with sympathy and empathy, kids cultivate a feeling of profound prosperity inside the relational intricacy.

The investigation of tending to normal difficulties consolidates the idea of tending to likely opposition or evasion in examining delicate points. Maturing guardians might show opposition or aversion with regards to specific subjects, maybe because of distress or dread. The aide urges youngsters to move toward these circumstances with persistence, delicate perseverance, and a readiness to make a continuous and agreeable space for conversations. By tending to opposition with understanding, youngsters add to a more open and cooperative correspondence dynamic.

Urgent to the conversation is the investigation of potential difficulties connected with protection and independence. Maturing guardians might esteem their security and independence in direction, and conversations about delicate points might address these angles. The aide perceives the significance of regarding guardians' limits and independence while as yet working with open correspondence. Kids are urged to track down an equilibrium that respects their folks' security while guaranteeing that significant subjects are tended to with the vital consideration and thought.

Besides, the aide digs into the test of addressing youngsters' own apprehensions and tensions connected with touchy subjects. Kids might hold onto fears or nerves about the maturing system, providing care liabilities, or the possible loss of their folks. The aide underscores the meaning of mindfulness and urges youngsters to investigate and address their own feelings prior to participating in delicate discussions. By recognizing and dealing with their feelings of dread, youngsters approach conversations with a more noteworthy profound versatility and status to help their maturing guardians.

The investigation of tending to normal difficulties integrates the idea of starting conversations at the fitting time and setting. Timing and climate assume a urgent part in the progress of delicate discussions. The aide proposes that kids pick minutes when the two they and their folks are loose, agreeable, and liberated from interruptions. By choosing proper times and settings, youngsters make a climate helpful for open and centered correspondence.

Vital to the conversation is the investigation of the expected test of tending to mental deterioration in maturing guardians. Mental changes might present difficulties in articulating considerations, communicating inclinations, or simply deciding.

The aide urges kids to move toward discussions with versatility, utilizing clear and straightforward language, and permitting additional time for their folks to impart. By tending to mental deterioration with persistence and understanding, youngsters add to a correspondence dynamic that obliges the interesting necessities of their maturing guardians.

Besides, the aide dives into the test of tending to possible struggles or conflicts during delicate conversations. Varying points of view might prompt struggles, and kids are urged to move toward these circumstances with compassion, undivided attention, and a guarantee to tracking down commonly pleasing arrangements. By exploring clashes with deference and understanding, youngsters add to a correspondence climate that encourages goal and keeps up with the strength of the parent-kid relationship.

The investigation of tending to normal difficulties consolidates the idea of offering educational help. Touchy themes might include complex data, and maturing guardians might profit from extra assets or backing. The aide proposes that youngsters can offer enlightening help by investigating significant subjects, sharing instructive materials, or interfacing their folks with experts who can offer direction. By offering enlightening help, youngsters engage their folks with the information expected to pursue informed choices.

Vital to the conversation is the investigation of potential difficulties connected with end-of-life arranging and conversations. End-of-life discussions can be especially delicate, and kids are urged to move toward these conversations with most extreme sympathy and compassion. The aide stresses the significance of making a space where maturing guardians feel open to communicating their desires and inclinations for end-of-life care. By tending to these difficulties with responsiveness, kids add to a providing care approach that praises their folks' independence and guarantees that their desires are regarded.

Besides, the aide dives into the test of tending to monetary worries or choices. Funds can be a sensitive subject, and kids are urged to move toward conversations with straightforwardness, compassion, and an emphasis on cooperative navigation. The aide recommends that kids can look for proficient exhortation if necessary and work along with their folks to make a monetary arrangement that lines up with their folks' qualities and needs. By tending to monetary worries with care, youngsters add to a correspondence dynamic that advances monetary prosperity and security for their maturing guardians.

The investigation of tending to normal difficulties integrates the idea of offering profound help during delicate discussions. Everyday encouragement is pivotal, particularly while talking about subjects that bring areas of strength for out. The aide urges youngsters to offer a listening ear, express sympathy, and approve their folks' sentiments. By offering close to home help, kids make a steady space where their maturing guardians feel comprehended, really focused on, and sincerely upheld.

Vital to the conversation is the investigation of potential difficulties connected with providing care liabilities. Conversations about providing care might include choices about living game plans, medical services choices, or the division of providing care liabilities among relatives. The aide underlines the significance of moving toward these conversations cooperatively, with an emphasis on shared liabilities, open correspondence, and a guarantee to guaranteeing the prosperity of the maturing guardian. By tending to providing care difficulties with cooperation, kids add to a providing care dynamic that is comprehensive and steady.

Also, the aide digs into the test of tending to expected sensations of culpability or weight that might emerge in maturing guardians. Maturing guardians might encounter sensations of culpability or weight related with their requirements or providing care liabilities. The aide urges youngsters to address these feelings with empathy, consolation, and an accentuation on the worth of common help inside the family. By tending to sensations of culpability, youngsters add to a correspondence climate that encourages profound prosperity and understanding.

The investigation of tending to normal difficulties consolidates the idea of including the whole family in conversations when proper. Relational peculiarities assume a critical part in delicate discussions, and the aide recommends that including the whole family when suitable can give different viewpoints, support, and cooperative direction. By encouraging family inclusion, youngsters add to a correspondence dynamic that values aggregate information and shared liability.

Critical to the conversation is the investigation of the expected test of overseeing expectant distress. Expectant anguish might emerge as kids expect changes in their folks' wellbeing or prosperity. The aide recognizes the intricacy of expectant despondency and urges kids to look for basic reassurance, express their sentiments, and participate in taking care of oneself. By tending to expectant misery with empathy, kids add to a correspondence dynamic that recognizes the close to home intricacies of the providing care venture.

Besides, the aide digs into the test of tending to changes in family jobs and elements. As guardians age, jobs inside the family might move, and youngsters are urged to move toward these progressions with flexibility and open correspondence. The aide accentuates the significance of perceiving and regarding the developing jobs of every relative, guaranteeing that correspondence mirrors the liquid idea of relational peculiarities. By tending to changes in jobs with understanding, youngsters add to a correspondence climate that values adaptability and common help.

The investigation of tending to normal difficulties integrates the idea of looking for outer help when required. In testing circumstances, youngsters might profit from looking for outside help, whether from help gatherings, advocates, or experts work in senior consideration. The aide stresses the benefit of connecting for help, recognizing that outside help can give direction, assets, and a current more extensive point of view on the difficulties. By looking for outer help, kids guarantee that they have the assets expected to explore complex circumstances with flexibility and care.

Significant to the conversation is the investigation of the expected test of offsetting straightforwardness with awareness. Finding some kind of harmony among straightforwardness and responsiveness is fundamental in touchy discussions. The aide urges youngsters to convey transparently while being aware of their folks' feelings and solace levels. By finding this equilibrium, kids cultivate a climate where data is imparted to clearness and empathy, guaranteeing that conversations stay conscious and kind.

Besides, the aide digs into the test of addressing likely misguided judgments or fears connected with maturing. Maturing guardians might hold onto fears or confusions about their own requirements or the effect on their youngsters. The aide urges youngsters to address these worries with sympathy, giving consolation, and offering clear data to disperse confusions. By tending to fears with understanding, kids add to a correspondence dynamic that encourages a feeling of safety and trust.

# Chapter 5

Creating Cherished Memories

Inside the endearing aide, "Together Through Time: A Kids' Manual for Esteeming Maturing Guardians," the part on "Making Valued Recollections" unfurls as an embroidery of warmth and association. This section digs into the extraordinary force of shared encounters, empowering youngsters to wind around snapshots of bliss, chuckling, and association into the texture of their relationship with maturing guardians. By encouraging a climate where esteemed recollections are made, kids add to a rich and persevering through embroidery that winds around together the past, present, and future.

The investigation starts with an affirmation of the significant effect that common recollections can have on the parent-youngster relationship. The aide stresses that recollections act as a scaffold that interfaces ages, making a story that rises above time. By perceiving the meaning of shared recollections, kids are urged to effectively take part in making minutes that will be prized in the present as well as a heritage for what's to come.

Additionally, the aide digs into the idea of distinguishing significant exercises that line up with the interests and inclinations of maturing guardians. Every individual's advantages and interests are special, and the aide proposes that youngsters require some investment to find exercises that give pleasure to their folks.

Whether it's taking part in a most loved leisure activity, investigating nature, or getting a charge out of comprehensive developments, kids can make treasured recollections by taking an interest in exercises that reverberate with their folks' advantages.

Critical to the conversation of making valued recollections is the investigation of the likely effect of basic and ordinary minutes. The aide highlights that valued recollections can be tracked down in the effortlessness of daily existence. Kids are urged to see the value in the magnificence of conventional minutes, like sharing a dinner, going for a comfortable stroll, or participating in sincere discussions. By finding euphoria in the effortlessness of shared encounters, kids add to an assortment of recollections that catch the embodiment of their relationship with their maturing guardians.

Additionally, the aide dives into the test of adjusting exercises that take care of both the physical and close to home prosperity of maturing guardians. Significant exercises can envelop a scope of encounters that advance actual wellbeing, close to home association, and in general prosperity. The aide urges youngsters to consider a comprehensive methodology, consolidating exercises that take special care of the different necessities of their folks. Whether it's taking part in delicate activities, getting a charge out of snapshots of unwinding, or participating in imaginative pursuits, kids can make a balanced embroidery of recollections that sustains both the body and the soul.

The investigation of making treasured recollections integrates the idea of praising achievements and extraordinary events. Achievements, birthday celebrations, and unique events give significant chances to make enduring recollections. The aide proposes that youngsters can design insightful festivals, integrating components that hold wistful incentive for their folks. By celebrating achievements, kids add to an embroidery of recollections that mark critical minutes in the common excursion of life.

Critical to the conversation is the investigation of the possible effect of making customs and ceremonies. Customs and ceremonies act as anchors in the texture of everyday life, making a feeling of coherence and association. The aide urges kids to lay out customs that hold individual importance, whether it's a family assembling, an exceptional dinner, or a yearly excursion. By making customs, kids add to an embroidery of recollections that is woven with the strings of shared encounters and persevering through associations.

Also, the aide digs into the test of obliging changes in actual capacities or medical issue. Maturing guardians might encounter changes in actual capacities, and youngsters are urged to adjust exercises to oblige these changes. The aide recommends that youngsters investigate exercises that line up with their folks' abilities to ongoing, it are pleasant and agreeable to guarantee that the encounters. By adjusting exercises, kids add to an embroidery of recollections that mirrors a humane and kind way to deal with their folks' prosperity.

The investigation of making appreciated recollections consolidates the idea of archiving minutes through different means. The aide perceives the benefit of recording recollections through photographs, recordings, or composed reflections. Kids are urged to catch the pith of shared encounters, making a substantial record of the minutes that characterize their relationship with their maturing guardians. By recording recollections, kids add to an embroidery that lives in the present as well as turns into a valued heritage for a long time into the future.

Critical to the conversation is the investigation of the possible effect of embracing immediacy and experience. Unconstrained minutes and experiences can add a dynamic and blissful aspect to the embroidery of recollections. The aide urges youngsters to embrace suddenness, whether it's setting out on a spontaneous trip, having a go at something new, or making treat for their folks. By mixing a feeling of experience into shared encounters, kids add to an embroidery of recollections that is loaded up with the soul of investigation and satisfaction.

Besides, the aide digs into the test of adjusting individual and aggregate interests inside the family. Every relative might have extraordinary interests, and the aide proposes that youngsters find an equilibrium that obliges both individual and aggregate inclinations. By consolidating various exercises that take care of various interests, kids add to an embroidery of recollections that mirrors the variety and lavishness of the relational peculiarity.

The investigation of making treasured recollections consolidates the idea of cultivating intergenerational associations. Shared encounters that span ages make an embroidery of recollections that traverses the continuum of everyday life. The aide urges youngsters to include grandparents, extraordinary grandparents, or other more seasoned relatives in exercises that encourage intergenerational associations. Whether it's sharing stories, messing around, or taking part in cooperative ventures, kids add to an embroidery of recollections that rises above generational limits.

Urgent to the conversation is the investigation of the possible effect of offering thanks and appreciation. Offering thanks and appreciation for shared minutes adds a layer of profundity and warmth to the embroidery of recollections. The aide recommends that youngsters effectively convey their appreciation for the encounters they share with their maturing guardians. By communicating appreciation, youngsters add to an embroidery of recollections that is woven with the strings of adoration, affirmation, and sincere association.

Also, the aide dives into the test of exploring contrasting inclinations or constraints in exercises. Maturing guardians might have explicit inclinations or impediments in specific exercises, and the aide urges kids to be mindful and accommodating of these variables. By regarding their folks' inclinations and adjusting exercises to line up with their solace levels, kids add to an embroidery of recollections that mirrors a smart and caring way to deal with shared encounters.

The investigation of making esteemed recollections integrates the idea of investigating tactile rich encounters. Connecting with the faculties — whether through the enthusiasm for nature, relishing tasty dinners, or getting a charge out of music — adds a multi-faceted quality to shared encounters. The aide urges kids to investigate exercises that invigorate the faculties, making an embroidery of recollections that is rich with tactile impressions. By embracing tactile rich encounters, youngsters add to an embroidery that catches the magnificence and dynamic quality of life's tangible embroidery.

Significant to the conversation is the investigation of the likely effect of cultivating chuckling and satisfaction. Giggling and delight are strings that wind through the embroidered artwork of loved recollections. The aide proposes that youngsters effectively look for snapshots of giggling and bliss, whether through humor, shared jokes, or cheerful exercises. By cultivating chuckling and delight, kids add to an embroidery of recollections that is saturated with the glow and energy of shared bliss.

In addition, the aide dives into the test of obliging different energy levels or inclinations for action. Maturing guardians might have differing energy levels or inclinations for the speed of exercises, and the aide urges youngsters to track down an agreeable equilibrium. By choosing exercises that take care of various energy levels and inclinations, kids add to an embroidery of recollections that obliges the different requirements of all relatives.

The investigation of making appreciated recollections consolidates the idea of investigating social and significant tourist spots. Visiting social or significant milestones gives a chance to make recollections injected with importance and association. The aide urges kids to investigate places that hold individual or social importance for their folks, making an embroidery of recollections that mirrors the lavishness of legacy and shared history. By visiting social milestones, youngsters add to an embroidery that respects the roots and accounts that shape their family story.

Significant to the conversation is the investigation of the possible effect of intelligent minutes and narrating. Intelligent minutes and narrating add a story profundity to the embroidery of recollections. The aide proposes that kids take part in intelligent discussions, sharing stories, and accounts that catch the embodiment of their family's process. By integrating intelligent minutes, youngsters add to an embroidery of recollections that turns into a living story, went down through the ages.

Also, the aide digs into the test of exploring advancing interests and inclinations over the long haul. As people age, their inclinations and inclinations might develop, and the aide urges youngsters to adjust exercises to line up with these changes. By remaining receptive to the developing interests of their folks, youngsters add to an embroidery of recollections that mirrors the powerful idea of self-awareness and investigation.

The investigation of making esteemed recollections integrates the idea of esteeming the current second. Esteemed recollections are not restricted to the past; they are constantly being made in the present. The aide urges youngsters to esteem and completely submerge themselves right now, relishing the delight, association, and love that each common experience brings. By esteeming the present, kids add to an embroidery of recollections that is persistently unfurling, with every second adding to the lavishness of their common history.

Urgent to the conversation is the investigation of the possible effect of developing a disposition of appreciation. Appreciation fills in as an establishment for making valued recollections. The aide recommends that youngsters effectively develop a disposition of appreciation, appreciating the minutes they share with their maturing guardians. By embracing appreciation, kids add to an embroidery of recollections that is woven with the strings of appreciation, gratefulness, and a profound affirmation of the value of shared encounters.

In addition, the aide digs into the test of exploring advances and changes in relational peculiarities. Advances, whether connected with life stages, wellbeing, or family structures, may present changes in the elements of shared encounters. The aide urges youngsters to move toward advances with versatility and flexibility, tracking down ways of making new recollections that mirror the developing idea of their family process. By exploring changes with beauty, youngsters add to an embroidery of recollections that embraces the recurring pattern of life.

5.1 Encouraging children to spend quality time with their aging parents

Inside the caring aide, "Together Through Time: A Youngsters' Manual for Valuing Maturing Guardians," the section on "Empowering Kids to Invest Quality Energy with Their Maturing Guardians" unfurls as a strong investigation of the extraordinary force of shared minutes. This portion dives into the meaning of purposeful and significant time spent together, uplifting youngsters to develop a rich embroidery of recollections with their maturing guardians. By cultivating a climate where quality time comes first, youngsters add to a relationship that is sustained by the glow, association, and getting through bonds that characterize the intergenerational venture.

The investigation starts with an affirmation of the significant effect that quality time can have on the parent-youngster relationship. The aide underscores that time is a valuable and limited asset, and deliberate endeavors to get to know each other convey a special importance. By perceiving the worth of time, youngsters are urged to focus on snapshots of association, giggling, and shared encounters that make a groundwork of getting through recollections.

In addition, the aide dives into the idea of understanding and valuing the uniqueness of each parent-youngster relationship. Each parent-kid relationship is innately one of a kind, formed by shared history, encounters, and the complexities of individual characters. The aide recommends that kids require some investment to comprehend and value the particular characteristics of their relationship with each parent. By perceiving and praising these interesting elements, youngsters make a space where quality time turns into a customized and loved articulation of their association.

Significant to the conversation of empowering youngsters to invest quality energy is the investigation of the likely effect of undivided attention and presence. Quality time stretches out past simple actual presence; it includes undivided attention and veritable commitment. The aide urges youngsters to be completely present during shared minutes, listening mindfully, and establishing a climate where open correspondence thrives. By rehearsing undivided attention, youngsters add to a relationship that is extended by common figuring out, sympathy, and the wealth of shared discussions.

Also, the aide dives into the test of exploring occupied plans and contending needs. In the rushing about of day to day existence, kids might confront contending needs, like work, school, and individual responsibilities. The aide perceives the significance of finding an equilibrium and urges youngsters to cut out deliberate pockets of time for their maturing guardians. By focusing on quality time in the midst of occupied plans, kids add to a relationship that is supported by deliberate endeavors to sustain association and shared encounters.

The investigation of empowering kids to invest quality energy consolidates the idea of investigating shared interests and leisure activities. Shared interests and side interests give a significant setting to quality time spent together. The aide recommends that youngsters find exercises that line up with the interests of their maturing guardians, whether it's a common side interest, a most loved diversion, or another experience. By participating in exercises that reverberate with shared interests, kids add to a relationship that is enhanced by the delight of shared interests.

Significant to the conversation is the investigation of the likely effect of making a daily practice of value time. Laying out a daily schedule of value time encourages consistency and consistency in the parent-kid relationship. The aide urges youngsters to integrate standard snapshots of association into their schedules, whether it's a week after week feast, an assigned excursion, or everyday discussions. By making a daily practice of value time, youngsters add to a relationship that is secured by the solace and dependability of shared minutes.

In addition, the aide digs into the test of defeating generational holes and contrasts. Generational holes might introduce contrasts in points of view, interests, and correspondence styles. The aide perceives the significance of connecting these holes and urges youngsters to move toward their folks with receptiveness and an eagerness to grasp their novel perspectives. By exploring generational contrasts with deference and interest, kids add to a relationship that rises above generational limits, encouraging an association that is based on common regard and appreciation.

The investigation of empowering youngsters to invest quality energy integrates the idea of encouraging a comprehensive climate for shared exercises. Inclusivity guarantees that all relatives, including maturing guardians, feel esteemed and effectively took part in shared exercises. The aide recommends that kids consider the inclinations and solace levels of their folks while arranging exercises, establishing a comprehensive climate where everybody feels invited and included. By encouraging inclusivity, youngsters add to a relationship that is reinforced by a feeling of having a place and shared cooperation.

Significant to the conversation is the investigation of the likely effect of embracing innovation as an instrument for association. In the computerized age, innovation fills in as an important device for remaining associated, particularly when geological distances might be a variable. The aide urges kids to use innovation to work with virtual associations with their maturing guardians, whether through video calls, informing applications, or shared advanced encounters. By embracing innovation for the purpose of association, kids add to a relationship that rises above actual distances, encouraging a feeling of closeness and association.

Besides, the aide digs into the test of tending to wellbeing related concerns or impediments. Maturing guardians might confront wellbeing related provokes that influence their capacity to participate in specific exercises. The aide perceives the significance of moving toward these difficulties with awareness and versatility. Youngsters are urged to investigate exercises that line up with their folks' wellbeing needs, guaranteeing that the time spent together is pleasant and helpful for their prosperity. By adjusting exercises to oblige wellbeing related concerns, youngsters add to a relationship that focuses on the wellbeing and solace of their maturing guardians.

The investigation of empowering youngsters to invest quality energy integrates the idea of including other relatives. Relational intricacies assume a critical part in the parent-youngster relationship, and including other relatives makes a feeling of shared association. The aide recommends that youngsters think about family social affairs, reunions, or joint exercises that include different ages. By cultivating associations inside the more extensive family, kids add to a relationship that is improved by the aggregate warmth and backing of more distant family bonds.

Essential to the conversation is the investigation of the possible effect of arranging shocks or extraordinary events. Amazements and exceptional events add a component of pleasure and expectation to quality time spent together. The aide urges kids to design astonishes or remember extraordinary events that hold nostalgic incentive for their maturing guardians. By making paramount and unforeseen minutes, youngsters add to a relationship that is loaded up with the delight of shared shocks and significant festivals.

In addition, the aide digs into the test of tending to potential correspondence boundaries. Maturing guardians might confront correspondence hindrances, whether because of hearing misfortune, mental changes, or different variables. The aide perceives the significance of embracing compelling correspondence procedures, like talking plainly, utilizing visual guides, and rehearsing persistence. By tending to correspondence boundaries with versatility, youngsters add to a relationship that is supported by clear and obliging correspondence.

The investigation of empowering youngsters to invest quality energy integrates the idea of esteeming the variety of shared encounters. Each common experience, whether large or little, adds to the embroidered artwork of the parent-youngster relationship. The aide recommends that youngsters esteem the variety of shared encounters, appreciating the lavishness that comes from different minutes. By embracing the variety of shared encounters, youngsters add to a relationship that is layered with the profundity and surface of a large number of treasured recollections.

Critical to the conversation is the investigation of the expected effect of making a feeling of expectation for shared exercises. Expectation adds an intriguing and positive aspect to the experience of value time. The aide urges kids to make a feeling of expectation by arranging exercises ahead of time, examining impending excursions, or astonishing their folks with energizing plans. By imbuing a feeling of expectation, youngsters add to a relationship that is portrayed by the delight and energy of shared minutes.

In addition, the aide digs into the test of addressing expected opposition or hesitance to take part in exercises. Maturing guardians might display obstruction or hesitance to specific exercises, and the aide urges kids to move toward these circumstances with compassion and understanding. By investigating exercises that line up with their folks' solace levels and inclinations, youngsters add to a relationship that is based on common regard and an obliging way to deal with shared encounters.

The investigation of empowering kids to invest quality energy integrates the idea of making a harmony among individual and shared exercises. While shared exercises are significant, the aide perceives the significance of permitting space for individual pursuits and interests.

Youngsters are urged to figure out some kind of harmony that obliges both shared and individual time, regarding the independence and individual inclinations of their maturing guardians. By making an amicable equilibrium, youngsters add to a relationship that is portrayed by an insightful mix of shared and individual encounters.

Critical to the conversation is the investigation of the expected effect of intelligent minutes and appreciation. Intelligent minutes and articulations of appreciation add a layer of profundity and appreciation to quality time spent together. The aide recommends that kids effectively participate in intelligent discussions, sharing snapshots of appreciation for the time they enjoy with their maturing guardians. By integrating intelligent minutes and articulations of appreciation, youngsters add to a relationship that is improved by a significant affirmation of the worth and meaning of shared encounters.

Also, the aide dives into the test of tending to possible culpability or worries no time like the present limitations. Kids might encounter culpability or worries no time like the present imperatives, particularly assuming that they are adjusting various obligations. The aide urges youngsters to move toward these sentiments with self-empathy, perceiving that quality time is about deliberate minutes as opposed to amount. By exploring sensations of responsibility with understanding, youngsters add to a relationship that is supported by the certified and genuine nature of the time they share.

The investigation of empowering youngsters to invest quality energy integrates the idea of making a tradition of treasured minutes. Each common second adds to an inheritance that rises above time, turning into a loved account inside the family story. The aide recommends that youngsters effectively take part in the production of a heritage by sustaining significant associations, reporting shared encounters, and communicating affection and appreciation. By making a tradition of valued minutes, youngsters add to a relationship that stretches out past the present, turning into an immortal and getting through articulation of affection.

5.2 Suggesting activities that foster connection and joy

Inside the caring aide, "Together Through Time: A Youngsters' Manual for Esteeming Maturing Guardians," the section on "Recommending Exercises that Encourage Association and Bliss" unfurls as a lively investigation of significant and euphoric encounters. This fragment digs into a heap of exercises intended to encourage association, giggling, and shared minutes, underlining the extraordinary force of purposeful and connecting with collaborations among youngsters and their maturing guardians. By proposing exercises that deliver association and satisfaction, kids add to a relationship that is improved by the glow, essentialness, and getting through bonds that portray the intergenerational venture.

The investigation starts with an affirmation of the different scope of exercises that can support association and bliss. The aide perceives that each parent-youngster relationship is special, and exercises can be customized to mirror the common interests, inclinations, and elements of individual families. By valuing the variety of conceivable outcomes, kids are urged to investigate exercises that reverberate with the particular characteristics and securities they share with their maturing guardians.

Additionally, the aide digs into the idea of considering both physical and profound prosperity while recommending exercises. Significant exercises incorporate those that draw in the body as well as those that support the soul and feelings. The aide proposes that youngsters investigate a comprehensive way to deal with exercises, integrating components that advance actual wellbeing, profound association, and generally prosperity. By taking into account the exhaustive requirements of their folks, kids add to a rich embroidery of encounters that cultivates both physical and profound essentialness.

Significant to the conversation is the investigation of the expected effect of thinking back and narrating as exercises. Thinking back and narrating act as useful assets for association, permitting guardians and kids to share recollections, tales, and biographies. The aide urges youngsters to participate in exercises that work with thinking back, like glancing through old photograph collections, sharing family stories, or making memory boxes. By embracing memory as a movement, kids add to a relationship that is developed by the lavishness of shared stories and the festival of the family's aggregate history.

Additionally, the aide digs into the test of obliging different energy levels or inclinations for movement. Maturing guardians might have changing energy levels or inclinations for the speed of exercises, and the aide urges kids to track down an amicable equilibrium. By choosing exercises that take special care of various energy levels and inclinations, kids add to a relationship that obliges the different requirements of all relatives, encouraging a feeling of inclusivity and shared interest.

The investigation of recommending exercises that cultivate association and satisfaction integrates the idea of integrating human expressions into shared encounters. Innovative articulations through workmanship, music, or dance give a special road to association and satisfaction. The aide recommends that youngsters investigate exercises, for example, craftsmanship projects, melodic meetings, or dance exercises that line up with their folks' advantages. By integrating artistic expressions into shared encounters, youngsters add to a relationship that is imbued with innovativeness, self-articulation, and the delight of imaginative investigation.

Significant to the conversation is the investigation of the expected effect of nature-based exercises. Interfacing with nature fills in as a remedial and restoring experience, giving chances to shared snapshots of serenity and appreciation. The aide urges kids to investigate exercises, for example, nature strolls, planting, or picnics in regular settings. By embracing nature-based exercises, youngsters add to a relationship that is improved by the magnificence, serenity, and imparted association with the regular world.

Also, the aide dives into the test of tending to possible versatility or wellbeing related concerns. Maturing guardians might confront versatility or wellbeing related provokes that influence their capacity to participate in specific exercises. The aide perceives the significance of moving toward these difficulties with flexibility and thought. Youngsters are urged to investigate exercises that line up with their folks' wellbeing needs, guaranteeing that the encounters are charming and helpful for their prosperity. By adjusting exercises to oblige wellbeing related concerns, youngsters add to a relationship that focuses on the wellbeing and solace of their maturing guardians.

The investigation of recommending exercises that encourage association and satisfaction consolidates the idea of culinary encounters. Shared dinners, cooking meetings, or culinary experiences set out open doors for association and satisfaction around the eating table. The aide recommends that kids investigate exercises connected with cooking, attempting new recipes, or sharing most loved feasts. By taking part in culinary encounters, kids add to a relationship that is enhanced with the glow of shared feasts and the delight of culinary investigation.

Significant to the conversation is the investigation of the expected effect of intergenerational projects or cooperative undertakings. Joint ventures and cooperative undertakings give a feeling of motivation and accomplishment, encouraging association through shared objectives. The aide urges kids to leave on intergenerational projects, whether it's a family scrapbooking project, a Do-It-Yourself home improvement task, or an innovative undertaking. By taking part in cooperative undertakings, kids add to a relationship that is reinforced by a feeling of collaboration, achievement, and the delight of making together.

Additionally, the aide dives into the test of tending to potential correspondence obstructions. Maturing guardians might confront correspondence boundaries, whether because of hearing misfortune, mental changes, or different elements. The aide perceives the significance of embracing successful correspondence procedures, like utilizing visual guides, motions, or composed correspondence. By tending to correspondence hindrances with versatility, kids add to a relationship that is supported by clear and obliging correspondence, it are open and pleasant to guarantee that common exercises.

The investigation of recommending exercises that cultivate association and delight consolidates the idea of innovation empowered encounters. In the computerized age, innovation fills in as a significant device for making associations, particularly when actual distances might be a component. The aide proposes that youngsters influence innovation to work with virtual encounters with their maturing guardians, whether through video calls, web based games, or shared advanced exercises. By embracing innovation for the purpose of association, kids add to a relationship that rises above geological limits, cultivating a feeling of closeness and shared encounters.

Significant to the conversation is the investigation of the likely effect of proactive tasks that advance wellbeing and prosperity. Taking part in proactive tasks adds to actual wellbeing as well as gives amazing chances to shared snapshots of development and essentialness. The aide urges youngsters to investigate exercises like delicate activities, strolls, or yoga meetings that line up with their folks' actual capacities. By integrating proactive tasks, youngsters add to a relationship that focuses on the prosperity and imperativeness of their maturing guardians.

Besides, the aide dives into the test of addressing expected opposition or hesitance to take part in exercises. Maturing guardians might show obstruction or hesitance to specific exercises, and the aide urges youngsters to move toward these circumstances with sympathy and understanding. By investigating exercises that line up with their folks' solace levels and inclinations, youngsters add to a relationship that is based on common regard and an obliging way to deal with shared encounters.

The investigation of proposing exercises that encourage association and delight consolidates the idea of celebratory encounters. Extraordinary events, occasions, and family festivities give valuable chances to shared euphoria and association. The aide recommends that kids plan celebratory encounters, whether it's a birthday festivity, an occasion gathering, or a family get-together. By recognizing exceptional events, kids add to a relationship that is enhanced by the delight of shared festivals and the making of enduring recollections.

Urgent to the conversation is the investigation of the possible effect of music as a device for association and satisfaction. Music has the ability to summon feelings, make shared recollections, and act as a wellspring of bliss. The aide urges youngsters to integrate music into shared encounters, whether through paying attention to main tunes, playing instruments together, or going to shows. By embracing music as a device for association, youngsters add to a relationship that is blended by the common rhythms and songs of melodic encounters.

Besides, the aide dives into the test of tending to potential monetary imperatives while proposing exercises. Monetary contemplations might influence the sorts of exercises that are attainable, and the aide perceives the significance of tracking down practical and pleasant choices.

Youngsters are urged to investigate exercises that line up with their monetary requirements, it are available and agreeable to guarantee that common encounters. By being aware of monetary contemplations, youngsters add to a relationship that is supported by the straightforwardness and delight of shared minutes.

The investigation of proposing exercises that cultivate association and bliss integrates the idea of investigating social and significant tourist spots. Visiting social or significant milestones gives an amazing chance to make recollections mixed with importance and association. The aide recommends that youngsters investigate places that hold individual or social significance for their folks, setting out open doors for shared investigation and reflection. By visiting social milestones, youngsters add to a relationship that praises the roots and stories that shape their family story.

Urgent to the conversation is the investigation of the possible effect of care and unwinding exercises. Snapshots of care and unwinding make a quiet and quieting climate, cultivating a feeling of serenity and association. The aide urges youngsters to investigate exercises like contemplation, delicate yoga, or unwinding meetings that advance a quiet climate. By integrating care into shared encounters, kids add to a relationship that is grounded in snapshots of serenity and shared quiet.

Also, the aide dives into the test of exploring possible generational holes or contrasts in interests. Generational holes might introduce contrasts in points of view, interests, and inclinations. The aide perceives the significance of figuring out some shared interest and urges youngsters to investigate exercises that span generational contrasts. By embracing shared interests and finding exercises that reverberate with the two ages, youngsters add to a relationship that is enhanced by the variety and wealth of intergenerational associations.

5.3 Emphasizing the value of creating lasting memories

Inside the sincere aide, "Together Through Time: A Youngsters' Manual for Treasuring Maturing Guardians," the section on "Stressing the Benefit of Making Enduring Recollections" unfurls as a strong investigation of the persevering through meaning of shared encounters. This fragment digs into the significant effect of purposeful memory-production, empowering kids to perceive the worth and magnificence in winding around an embroidery of minutes that rise above time. By underlining the significance of making enduring recollections, youngsters add to a relationship that is improved by the glow, profundity, and immortal associations that characterize the intergenerational venture.

The investigation starts with an affirmation of the groundbreaking force of recollections. Recollections act as the strings that wind around together the texture of the parent-kid relationship, making a story that traverses ages. The aide underlines that recollections are not momentary; they are getting through engraves that shape the character of a family. By perceiving the worth of recollections, kids are urged to effectively take part in the deliberate formation of minutes that will become treasured sections of their common history.

Also, the aide digs into the idea of grasping the meaning of the current second. Making enduring recollections is definitely not a far off try yet a demonstration of embracing and esteeming the present. The aide proposes that youngsters develop an attention to the current second, enjoying the delight, association, and love that each common experience brings. By perceiving the meaning of the present, kids add to a relationship that is grounded in the lavishness of the present time and place.

Essential to the conversation of underlining the benefit of making enduring recollections is the investigation of the expected effect of appreciation and appreciation. Appreciation fills in as an establishment for loving recollections, adding a layer of profundity and wealth to shared encounters. The aide urges youngsters to effectively offer thanks for the minutes they share with their maturing guardians. By embracing appreciation, kids add to a relationship that is improved by a significant affirmation of the value of shared encounters.

In addition, the aide dives into the test of exploring likely interruptions or hecticness. In the rushing about of day to day existence, youngsters might experience interruptions or contending needs. The aide perceives the significance of viewing an equilibrium and supports kids as aware of the minutes that add to enduring recollections. By exploring interruptions with purposefulness, youngsters add to a relationship that is described by the cognizant development of significant minutes in the midst of life's hecticness.

The investigation of underscoring the benefit of making enduring recollections consolidates the idea of perceiving the uniqueness of each parent-kid relationship. Each parent-youngster relationship is an unmistakable embroidery, woven with shared history, encounters, and the subtleties of individual characters. The aide recommends that youngsters celebrate and value the uniqueness of their relationship with each parent. By perceiving and regarding this distinction, youngsters add to a relationship that is improved by the particular characteristics and bonds that characterize their association.

Pivotal to the conversation is the investigation of the possible effect of effectively taking part in shared encounters. Making enduring recollections includes dynamic cooperation at the times that unfurl.

The aide urges kids to be completely present during shared encounters, effectively captivating in discussions, exercises, and festivities. By partaking sincerely, kids add to a relationship that is molded by the wealth of their common presence and the shared interest in making significant minutes.

Additionally, the aide dives into the test of addressing expected hesitance or protection from taking part in memory-production exercises. Maturing guardians might show hesitance or protection from specific exercises, and the aide urges youngsters to move toward these circumstances with sympathy and understanding. By investigating exercises that line up with their folks' solace levels and inclinations, youngsters add to a relationship that is based on common regard and a chivalrous way to deal with shared encounters.

The investigation of stressing the benefit of making enduring recollections consolidates the idea of embracing the recurrent idea of life. Life unfurls in cycles, and the aide recommends that youngsters perceive the recurrent idea of encounters inside the family. By embracing the repeating excursion of life, kids add to a relationship that is portrayed by a comprehension of the interconnectedness of past, present, and future. The aide highlights that making enduring recollections isn't just a demonstration of adoration yet an acknowledgment of the continuous story that interfaces ages.

Pivotal to the conversation is the investigation of the possible effect of embracing suddenness and shock. Unconstrained minutes and amazements add a component of pleasure and delight to the production of enduring recollections. The aide urges kids to embrace suddenness, whether through impromptu excursions, shock festivities, or surprising motions.

By imbuing a feeling of shock into shared encounters, kids add to a relationship that is loaded up with the delight of startling minutes and the energy of unconstrained undertakings.

Besides, the aide dives into the test of tending to possible changes in wellbeing or actual capacities. Maturing guardians might encounter changes in wellbeing or actual capacities that influence their cooperation in specific exercises. The aide perceives the significance of adjusting exercises to oblige these changes. Youngsters are urged to investigate exercises that line up with their folks' abilities to ongoing, it are charming and agreeable to guarantee that the encounters. By adjusting exercises with thought for wellbeing and actual prosperity, kids add to a relationship that focuses on the solace and joy of their maturing guardians.

The investigation of underlining the benefit of making enduring recollections integrates the idea of recording minutes through different means. The aide perceives the meaning of archiving recollections through photographs, recordings, or composed reflections.

Youngsters are urged to catch the quintessence of shared encounters, making an unmistakable record of the minutes that characterize their relationship with their maturing guardians. By recording recollections, youngsters add to a relationship that lives in the present as well as turns into a valued heritage for a long time into the future.

Urgent to the conversation is the investigation of the possible effect of including other relatives in memory-production exercises. Relational peculiarities assume an essential part in the formation of enduring recollections, and the aide proposes that youngsters include other relatives in shared encounters. Whether through family get-togethers, reunions, or joint exercises, including more distant family individuals makes a feeling of aggregate association and shared interest. By cultivating associations inside the more extensive family, kids add to a relationship that is enhanced by the aggregate warmth and backing of more distant family bonds.

Besides, the aide dives into the test of tending to potential monetary limitations while making enduring recollections. Monetary contemplations might influence the sorts of exercises that are doable, and the aide perceives the significance of tracking down financially savvy and agreeable choices. Youngsters are urged to investigate exercises that line up with their monetary imperatives, guaranteeing that memory-production encounters are open and charming. By being aware of monetary contemplations, youngsters add to a relationship that is supported by the effortlessness and delight of shared minutes.

The investigation of stressing the benefit of making enduring recollections consolidates the idea of investigating customs and ceremonies. Customs and ceremonies give a feeling of coherence and shared history inside a family. The aide proposes that youngsters investigate and make customs that hold individual or social significance for their folks. By taking part in customs, kids add to a relationship that is woven with the strings of coherence, cultivating a feeling of association with the past while making new recollections for what's in store.

Critical to the conversation is the investigation of the likely effect of considering the inclinations and solace levels of maturing guardians. The aide urges youngsters to be sensitive to the inclinations and solace levels of their maturing guardians while arranging memory-production exercises. By taking into account these variables, youngsters establish a climate where their folks feel esteemed and open to, guaranteeing that the minutes shared are agreeable and significant. By regarding the singular requirements of their folks, youngsters add to a relationship that is portrayed by mindfulness and thought.

In addition, the aide digs into the test of tending to potential correspondence boundaries. Maturing guardians might confront correspondence boundaries, whether because of hearing misfortune, mental changes, or different variables.

The aide perceives the significance of taking on powerful correspondence methodologies, like utilizing visual guides, signals, or composed correspondence. By tending to correspondence boundaries with flexibility, youngsters add to a relationship that is supported by clear and obliging correspondence, guaranteeing that the most common way of making enduring recollections is comprehensive and pleasant for all.

The investigation of underlining the benefit of making enduring recollections integrates the idea of investigating different and comprehensive exercises. Inclusivity guarantees that all relatives, including maturing guardians, feel esteemed and effectively took part in memory-production exercises. The aide recommends that kids consider the inclinations and solace levels of their folks while arranging exercises, establishing a comprehensive climate where everybody feels invited and included. By encouraging inclusivity, youngsters add to a relationship that is reinforced by a feeling of having a place and shared interest.

Urgent to the conversation is the investigation of the possible effect of reflection and narrating in the making of enduring recollections. Reflection and narrating add a story profundity to the embroidery of recollections. The aide recommends that youngsters take part in intelligent discussions, sharing stories, and accounts that catch the quintessence of their family's process. By integrating intelligent minutes, youngsters add to a relationship that turns into a living story, went down through the ages. Narrating adds a layer of lavishness to the recollections made, permitting them to be shared and valued across time.

In addition, the aide digs into the test of exploring developing interests and inclinations after some time. As people age, their inclinations and inclinations might develop, and the aide urges youngsters to adjust memory-production exercises to line up with these changes. By remaining receptive to the developing interests of their folks, youngsters add to a relationship that is adaptable and receptive to the powerful idea of self-awareness and investigation.

# Chapter 6

Navigating Challenges

Inside the caring aide, "Together Through Time: A Youngsters' Manual for Loving Maturing Guardians," the section on "Exploring Difficulties" unfurls as a smart investigation of the intricacies that might emerge in the parent-kid relationship as guardians age. This fragment digs into the nuanced parts of providing care, close to home elements, and the different difficulties that kids might experience. By exploring these difficulties with sympathy, understanding, and useful procedures, kids add to a relationship that is invigorated by strength, empathy, and persevering through securities.

The investigation starts with an affirmation of the multi-layered nature of maturing and its effect on the two guardians and youngsters. Maturing is a characteristic piece of life, yet it accompanies its own arrangement of difficulties. The aide underlines that understanding the maturing system is fundamental for youngsters as they explore the progressions in their folks. By perceiving the certainty of maturing and its likely difficulties, youngsters are better prepared to move toward the excursion with compassion and a proactive mentality.

Besides, the aide dives into the idea of recognizing and tending to wellbeing related concerns. Maturing frequently achieves wellbeing difficulties, and youngsters might end up in the job of offering help and care. The aide recommends that youngsters effectively take part in discussions about their folks' wellbeing, remaining informed about ailments, medicines, and any possible impediments. By adopting a proactive strategy to wellbeing related concerns, youngsters add to a relationship that is portrayed by open correspondence and a common obligation to prosperity.

Essential to the conversation of exploring difficulties is the investigation of likely opposition or hesitance from maturing guardians. Guardians might oppose recognizing their changing requirements or might be hesitant to acknowledge help. The aide urges kids to move toward these circumstances with awareness, regard, and open correspondence. By cultivating a climate where guardians feel appreciated and comprehended, youngsters add to a relationship that is described by common regard and cooperative critical thinking.

In addition, the aide digs into the test of offsetting providing care liabilities with other life requests. Youngsters who take on providing care jobs might wind up shuffling numerous obligations, including work, individual life, and their own prosperity. The aide perceives the significance of tracking down an equilibrium and urges kids to lay out practical assumptions, look for help when required, and focus on taking care of oneself. By recognizing the intricacies of providing care and embracing a reasonable methodology, youngsters add to a relationship that is supported by their own prosperity and versatility.

The investigation of exploring difficulties consolidates the idea of tending to profound and mental parts of maturing. Maturing can achieve inner difficulties for the two guardians and youngsters, including sensations of misfortune, sorrow, or tension about what's in store. The aide proposes that youngsters approach these profound viewpoints with compassion and open correspondence. By making a place of refuge for profound articulation, kids add to a relationship that is described by mutual perspective and basic encouragement.

Significant to the conversation is the investigation of the likely effect of monetary contemplations on providing care. The monetary parts of providing care can be perplexing, and youngsters might have to explore issues connected with planning, clinical costs, or long haul care arranging. The aide urges kids to proactively talk about monetary issues with their folks, investigate accessible assets, and look for proficient exhortation when required. By tending to monetary contemplations with straightforwardness and joint effort, youngsters add to a relationship that is grounded in reasonable arrangements and a common obligation to monetary prosperity.

In addition, the aide digs into the test of understanding and regarding the independence of maturing guardians. Maturing guardians might esteem their freedom and independence, and kids need to explore this perspective with care. The aide recommends that kids take part in open discussions about their folks' inclinations, wants, and the degree of help they are happy with getting. By regarding the independence of maturing guardians, youngsters add to a relationship that is portrayed by a cooperative and circumspect way to deal with providing care.

The investigation of exploring difficulties consolidates the idea of tending to potential correspondence obstructions. Maturing may achieve changes in correspondence capacities, and youngsters might have to adjust their correspondence styles in like manner. The aide urges kids to show restraint, utilize clear and basic language, and investigate elective specialized strategies if vital. By tending to correspondence obstructions with flexibility, kids add to a relationship that is supported by clear and chivalrous correspondence, guaranteeing that the association stays solid.

Significant to the conversation is the investigation of the possible effect of geographic distances on providing care. In the present globalized world, kids might end up living in various areas from their maturing guardians. The aide proposes that youngsters investigate ways of remaining associated, whether through normal correspondence, virtual visits, or coordination with neighborhood encouraging groups of people. By utilizing innovation and encouraging associations across distances, youngsters add to a relationship that rises above geological limits, guaranteeing that the providing care venture is a common and cooperative exertion.

Also, the aide digs into the test of exploring developing jobs and elements inside the family. As guardians age, jobs and elements inside the family might move, and youngsters might wind up in new providing care jobs. The aide perceives the significance of adjusting to these progressions with adaptability, understanding, and continuous correspondence. By exploring developing jobs with beauty and responsiveness, kids add to a relationship that is portrayed by a dynamic and steady family structure.

The investigation of exploring difficulties integrates the idea of investigating lawful and end-of-life contemplations. Discussions about legitimate matters and end-of-life inclinations can be testing yet are fundamental for guaranteeing that the desires of maturing guardians are regarded. The aide recommends that kids take part in transparent conversations about authoritative archives, like wills and advance orders, and look for proficient direction when required. By tending to these contemplations with care and prescience, kids add to a relationship that is grounded in regard for their folks' desires and a smart way to deal with future preparation.

Vital to the conversation is the investigation of the likely effect of social or generational contrasts on providing care draws near. Social and generational elements might impact perspectives towards maturing and providing care. The aide urges kids to move toward these distinctions with interest, liberality, and an eagerness to grasp their folks' points of view. By exploring social and generational subtleties with deference, kids add to a relationship that is described by social responsiveness and a common appreciation for different points of view.

Besides, the aide dives into the test of tending to expected sensations of responsibility or deficiency in providing care. Youngsters might encounter sensations of culpability or insufficiency, particularly on the off chance that they see that they are not doing what's needed for their maturing guardians. The aide perceives the significance of self-sympathy and urges kids to recognize and address these sentiments with help from companions, family, or experts. By exploring sensations of responsibility with understanding and self-sympathy, youngsters add to a relationship that is supported by their own profound prosperity.

The investigation of exploring difficulties integrates the idea of looking for outside help and assets. Providing care can be requesting, and youngsters might profit from getting to outer encouraging groups of people, local area assets, or expert help. The aide proposes that kids investigate accessible help administrations, draw in with neighborhood parental figure gatherings, and look for direction from medical services experts. By looking for outside help, youngsters add to a relationship that is supported by an organization of care and help, guaranteeing that the providing care venture is shared and reasonable.

Urgent to the conversation is the investigation of the likely effect of kin elements on providing care liabilities. Kin elements might assume a critical part in providing care, and the aide urges youngsters to cultivate open correspondence and coordinated effort with kin. By cooperating and conveying liabilities in light of individual qualities and accessibility, youngsters add to a relationship that is portrayed by shared providing care liabilities and common help.

Besides, the aide digs into the test of tending to likely struggles or conflicts inside the family. Providing care liabilities might bring about clashes or conflicts among relatives, and the aide perceives the significance of resolving these issues with compassion and open correspondence. By encouraging a culture of understanding and split the difference, youngsters add to a relationship that is strong despite challenges and described by a common obligation to the prosperity of their maturing guardians.

The investigation of exploring difficulties consolidates the idea of encouraging versatility and flexibility. The providing care venture is innately unique, and unanticipated difficulties might emerge.

The aide recommends that youngsters develop flexibility and versatility, embracing an outlook that is available to getting the hang of, changing procedures, and tracking down clever fixes. By encouraging strength, youngsters add to a relationship that is described by a persevering through capacity to explore difficulties with elegance and assurance.

Significant to the conversation is the investigation of the possible effect of making a strong and cooperative providing care plan. The aide urges youngsters to work cooperatively with their folks to make a providing care plan that lines up with their folks' inclinations, needs, and wants. By including guardians in the dynamic cycle, youngsters add to a relationship that is portrayed by shared responsibility for providing care venture and a cooperative way to deal with tending to difficulties.

In addition, the aide dives into the test of tending to expected sensations of close to home burnout or weariness. Providing care liabilities might be sincerely requesting, and kids might encounter sensations of burnout or fatigue. The aide perceives the significance of taking care of oneself, defining limits, and looking for rest when required. By focusing on their own prosperity, kids add to a relationship that is supported by their close to home flexibility and the ability to give care empathy.

The investigation of exploring difficulties consolidates the idea of encouraging open correspondence with guardians about their inclinations for care. The aide proposes that kids participate in continuous discussions with their folks about their inclinations for care, living courses of action, and different parts of maturing. By keeping up with open correspondence, youngsters add to a relationship that is described by a common perspective of their folks' desires and a cooperative way to deal with navigation.

Urgent to the conversation is the investigation of the expected effect of integrating innovation into providing care. Innovation can act as an important instrument for correspondence, observing wellbeing, and getting to help administrations. The aide urges youngsters to investigate innovative arrangements that can improve providing care, for example, telehealth administrations, wellbeing checking applications, or correspondence stages. By utilizing innovation, kids add to a relationship that is portrayed by current and productive providing care rehearses.

In addition, the aide dives into the test of tending to expected sensations of anguish or expectant distress. Kids might encounter sensations of anguish as they witness the progressions in their maturing guardians. The aide perceives the significance of recognizing and handling these sentiments with help from companions, family, or experts. By exploring sensations of pain with sympathy and understanding, kids add to a relationship that is supported by profound credibility and shared affirmation of the intricacies of maturing.

6.1 Discussing common challenges that may arise in caring for aging parents

Inside the shrewd aide, "Together Through Time: A Youngsters' Manual for Loving Maturing Guardians," the section on "Examining Normal Difficulties in Focusing on Maturing Guardians" unfurls as an empathetic investigation of the obstacles and intricacies that kids might experience while really focusing on their maturing guardians. This fragment digs into the nuanced parts of providing care, revealing insight into normal difficulties and offering techniques for tending to them with sympathy and reasonableness. By straightforwardly examining these difficulties, youngsters can explore the providing care venture with versatility, understanding, and a guarantee to supporting the prosperity of their maturing guardians.

The investigation starts with an affirmation of the multi-layered nature of the maturing system. Maturing is a characteristic piece of life, yet it achieves a range of changes, both physical and close to home. The aide underscores that understanding the different components of maturing is essential for youngsters as they set out on the providing care venture. By perceiving the diverse idea of maturing, youngsters can approach providing care with a comprehensive comprehension, tending to the actual perspectives as well as the profound and mental aspects.

Also, the aide digs into the idea of distinguishing and tending to wellbeing related concerns. Maturing frequently accompanies an improved probability of medical problems, going from persistent circumstances to progress in years related illnesses. The aide proposes that youngsters effectively participate in discussions about their folks' wellbeing, keeping up with open lines of correspondence with medical care experts, and remaining informed about possible difficulties. By proactively tending to wellbeing related concerns, youngsters add to a relationship that is grounded in a common obligation to the prosperity of their maturing guardians.

Pivotal to the conversation of normal difficulties is the investigation of the expected effect of mental changes in maturing guardians. Mental degradation, whether because of normal maturing or conditions like dementia, presents a novel arrangement of difficulties. The aide urges youngsters to move toward mental changes with persistence, understanding, and a pledge to keeping up with the nobility and independence of their folks. By adjusting correspondence styles, establishing strong conditions, and looking for proficient direction when important, youngsters add to a relationship that tends to mental changes with sympathy and care.

Additionally, the aide dives into the test of offsetting providing care liabilities with other life requests. Youngsters who take on providing care jobs frequently end up exploring a sensitive harmony between work, individual life, and their own prosperity.

The aide perceives the significance of laying out sensible assumptions, defining limits, and focusing on taking care of oneself. By recognizing the intricacies of offsetting providing care with other life requests, kids add to a relationship that is described by a feasible and adjusted way to deal with providing care.

The investigation of normal difficulties in focusing on maturing guardians consolidates the idea of tending to portability and actual restrictions.

Maturing may achieve changes in versatility and actual capacities, affecting day to day exercises and schedules. The aide proposes that youngsters adjust living spaces to oblige these changes, investigate assistive gadgets, and empower proactive tasks that line up with their folks' capacities. By tending to versatility and actual impediments with flexibility and thought, kids add to a relationship that focuses on the solace and freedom of their maturing guardians.

Pivotal to the conversation is the investigation of the expected effect of profound and mental difficulties in the two guardians and kids. Maturing can inspire a scope of feelings, including sensations of misfortune, uneasiness, or sorrow. The aide urges kids to move toward these close to home perspectives with sympathy, cultivating open correspondence and establishing a strong climate for profound articulation. By tending to close to home and mental difficulties with responsiveness, youngsters add to a relationship that is portrayed by common perspective and daily reassurance.

Additionally, the aide digs into the test of tending to expected obstruction or hesitance from maturing guardians. Guardians might oppose recognizing their changing requirements or might be hesitant to acknowledge help. The aide urges youngsters to move toward these circumstances with persistence, regard, and open correspondence. By encouraging a climate where guardians feel appreciated and comprehended, youngsters add to a relationship that is portrayed by common regard and cooperative critical thinking.

The investigation of normal difficulties in focusing on maturing guardians consolidates the idea of monetary contemplations. The monetary parts of providing care can be perplexing, including clinical costs, long haul care arranging, and likely acclimations to monetary courses of action. The aide recommends that kids participate in open conversations about monetary issues with their folks, investigate accessible assets, and look for proficient guidance when required. By tending to monetary contemplations with straightforwardness and coordinated effort, kids add to a relationship that is grounded in down to earth arrangements and a common obligation to monetary prosperity.

Pivotal to the conversation is the investigation of the expected effect of kin elements on providing care liabilities. Kin might have alternate points of view, accessibility, and jobs in providing care, prompting likely struggles or lopsided characteristics in obligations.

The aide urges kids to encourage open correspondence and joint effort with kin, guaranteeing that providing care liabilities are appropriated in light of individual qualities and accessibility. By cooperating and recognizing the extraordinary commitments of every kin, kids add to a relationship that is portrayed by shared providing care liabilities and common help.

Additionally, the aide digs into the test of exploring developing jobs and elements inside the family. As guardians age, jobs and elements might move, prompting possible changes in family connections. The aide perceives the significance of adjusting to these progressions with adaptability, understanding, and continuous correspondence. By exploring developing jobs with elegance and responsiveness, youngsters add to a relationship that is portrayed by a dynamic and steady family structure.

The investigation of normal difficulties in focusing on maturing guardians consolidates the idea of tending to likely sensations of culpability or deficiency. Kids might encounter sensations of responsibility, particularly in the event that they see that they are not doing what's necessary for their maturing guardians. The aide perceives the significance of self-empathy and urges youngsters to recognize and address these sentiments with help from companions, family, or experts. By exploring sensations of culpability with understanding and self-sympathy, kids add to a relationship that is supported by their own close to home prosperity.

Urgent to the conversation is the investigation of the expected effect of legitimate and end-of-life contemplations. Discussions about legitimate matters and end-of-life inclinations can be touchy however are fundamental for guaranteeing that the desires of maturing guardians are regarded. The aide recommends that kids take part in transparent conversations about authoritative reports, like wills and advance mandates, and look for proficient direction when required. By tending to these contemplations with care and prescience, youngsters add to a relationship that is grounded in regard for their folks' desires and a smart way to deal with future preparation.

Also, the aide digs into the test of tending to expected clashes or conflicts inside the family. Providing care liabilities might lead to clashes or conflicts among relatives, and the aide perceives the significance of resolving these issues with sympathy and open correspondence. By encouraging a culture of understanding and split the difference, kids add to a relationship that is strong despite challenges and portrayed by a common obligation to the prosperity of their maturing guardians.

The investigation of normal difficulties in focusing on maturing guardians consolidates the idea of looking for outside help and assets. Providing care can be requesting, and youngsters might profit from getting to outside help organizations, local area assets, or expert help.

The aide recommends that youngsters investigate accessible help administrations, draw in with nearby guardian gatherings, and look for direction from medical care experts. By looking for outer help, kids add to a relationship that is supported by an organization of care and help, guaranteeing that the providing care venture is shared and maintainable.

Essential to the conversation is the investigation of the likely effect of tending to potential correspondence boundaries. Maturing guardians might confront correspondence obstructions, whether because of hearing misfortune, mental changes, or different variables. The aide urges youngsters to show restraint, utilize clear and straightforward language, and investigate elective specialized techniques if important. By tending to correspondence boundaries with versatility, kids add to a relationship that is supported by clear and kind correspondence, guaranteeing that the association stays solid.

Also, the aide digs into the test of tending to expected changes in living game plans. Maturing guardians might confront choices about where and how they need to reside as their requirements advance. The aide recommends that youngsters participate in open conversations about living courses of action, investigating choices that line up with their folks' inclinations and requirements. By including guardians in these choices and regarding their independence, youngsters add to a relationship that is portrayed by cooperative direction and an obliging way to deal with changing day to day environments.

The investigation of normal difficulties in focusing on maturing guardians consolidates the idea of tending to likely social or generational contrasts. Social and generational variables might impact perspectives towards maturing and providing care. The aide urges kids to move toward these distinctions with interest, liberality, and a readiness to grasp their folks' points of view. By exploring social and generational subtleties with deference, kids add to a relationship that is described by social responsiveness and a common appreciation for different viewpoints.

Vital to the conversation is the investigation of the expected effect of tending to likely sensations of melancholy or expectant misery. Youngsters might encounter sensations of pain as they witness the progressions in their maturing guardians. The aide perceives the significance of recognizing and handling these sentiments with help from companions, family, or experts. By exploring sensations of sadness with sympathy and understanding, youngsters add to a relationship that is supported by close to home validness and shared affirmation of the intricacies of maturing.

Additionally, the aide digs into the test of tending to likely sensations of burnout or fatigue. Providing care liabilities might be sincerely requesting, and youngsters might encounter sensations of burnout or weariness.

The aide perceives the significance of taking care of oneself, defining limits, and looking for reprieve when required. By focusing on their own prosperity, kids add to a relationship that is supported by their profound flexibility and the ability to give care sympathy.

6.2 Providing guidance on problem-solving and conflict resolution

Inside the humane aide, "Together Through Time: A Kids' Manual for Esteeming Maturing Guardians," the section on "Giving Direction on Critical thinking and Compromise" unfurls as a smart investigation of the techniques and approaches youngsters can utilize to explore difficulties, tackle issues, and address clashes with regards to really focusing on maturing guardians. This fragment digs into the subtleties of successful critical thinking and compromise, offering down to earth direction to cultivate correspondence, understanding, and strength. By embracing these techniques, youngsters add to a relationship that is strengthened by cooperative critical thinking, open correspondence, and a common obligation to the prosperity of their maturing guardians.

The investigation starts with an affirmation of the certainty of difficulties in the providing care venture. Really focusing on maturing guardians is a dynamic and complex obligation that might lead to different difficulties, going from wellbeing related worries to profound and commonsense issues. The aide stresses that comprehension and acknowledging the certainty of demands is a pivotal initial step. By recognizing difficulties as a characteristic piece of the providing care venture, youngsters can move toward critical thinking with a proactive and reasonable mentality.

Besides, the aide dives into the idea of cultivating open correspondence. Powerful critical thinking and compromise depend on clear and open correspondence. The aide recommends that youngsters develop a culture of open correspondence by effectively paying attention to their folks, offering their viewpoints and sentiments with trustworthiness, and empowering their folks to share their points of view. By cultivating open correspondence, youngsters add to a relationship that is portrayed by common comprehension and a common obligation to cooperative critical thinking.

Pivotal to the conversation of giving direction on critical thinking and compromise is the investigation of undivided attention abilities. Undivided attention includes completely focusing, understanding, answering, and recalling what is being said. The aide urges youngsters to rehearse undivided attention during discussions with their folks, guaranteeing that they fathom the words expressed as well as the feelings and subtleties hidden the correspondence. By improving undivided attention abilities, youngsters add to a relationship that is reinforced by a profound comprehension of their folks' requirements, concerns, and points of view.

In addition, the aide underscores the significance of compassion in critical thinking. Sympathy includes understanding and talking about the thoughts of another. The aide proposes that youngsters come at the situation from their folks' perspective, taking into account their viewpoints, feelings, and encounters. By moving toward critical thinking with sympathy, kids add to a relationship that is described by empathy and a certifiable comprehension of the difficulties and feelings their folks might confront.

The investigation of giving direction on critical thinking and compromise consolidates the idea of recognizing shared objectives. Cooperative critical thinking is best when all gatherings included share shared objectives and targets. The aide proposes that kids and their folks cooperate to recognize shared objectives connected with wellbeing, prosperity, and personal satisfaction. By adjusting on normal targets, kids add to a relationship that is joined in reason, encouraging a feeling of cooperation and shared obligation to accomplishing good results.

Pivotal to the conversation is the investigation of the possible effect of keeping a positive and arrangement situated mentality. Critical thinking is intrinsically attached to outlook, and the aide urges kids to move toward difficulties with a positive and arrangement situated mentality. Rather than zeroing in exclusively on the troubles, youngsters are urged to investigate expected arrangements, options, and proactive advances. By keeping a positive outlook, kids add to a relationship that is portrayed by flexibility and a resolute faith in the chance of tracking down valuable arrangements.

Also, the aide digs into the test of tending to possible contentions or conflicts with awareness and regard. Clashes might emerge in the providing care venture, and the aide perceives the significance of tending to these struggles with responsiveness and regard. Kids are urged to communicate their interests confidently yet strategically, keeping away from fault or analysis. By moving toward clashes with a circumspect and conscious disposition, youngsters add to a relationship that is portrayed by open correspondence and a common obligation to settling contrasts with generosity.

The investigation of giving direction on critical thinking and compromise integrates the idea of looking for split the difference and figuring out some shared interest. Compelling compromise frequently includes finding compromises that oblige the necessities and inclinations of all gatherings included. The aide proposes that youngsters and their folks investigate areas of shared view, look for compromise when vital, and find arrangements that are OK to everybody. By embracing split the difference, youngsters add to a relationship that is described by adaptability and a cooperative way to deal with settling contrasts.

Pivotal to the conversation is the investigation of the possible effect of looking for outer help when required. A few difficulties might require outside mastery or help, and the aide urges kids to look for help from medical services experts, guides, or care groups. By perceiving when outer help is important and effectively looking for it, kids add to a relationship that is described by a complete and all encompassing way to deal with critical thinking and compromise.

Besides, the aide dives into the test of tending to expected profound parts of struggles. Clashes might inspire a scope of feelings, and the aide perceives the significance of tending to the close to home parts of conflicts. Kids are urged to establish a steady climate for close to home articulation, permitting both themselves and their folks to straightforwardly discuss their thoughts. By recognizing and tending to the close to home elements of struggles, kids add to a relationship that is described by a common obligation to profound prosperity and understanding.

The investigation of giving direction on critical thinking and compromise consolidates the idea of returning to and changing systems depending on the situation. Critical thinking is an iterative interaction, and the aide proposes that youngsters stay versatile and open to changing techniques in light of the developing necessities and conditions. By returning to and changing methodologies depending on the situation, youngsters add to a relationship that is described by a dynamic and responsive way to deal with critical thinking, guaranteeing that arrangements stay viable and pertinent.

Essential to the conversation is the investigation of the possible effect of making a cooperative providing care plan. A cooperative providing care plan includes effectively including the two youngsters and guardians in dynamic cycles connected with care, wellbeing, and everyday exercises. The aide urges kids to work cooperatively with their folks to make a providing care plan that lines up with their folks' inclinations, needs, and wants. By including guardians in the dynamic cycle, kids add to a relationship that is portrayed by shared responsibility for providing care venture and a cooperative way to deal with tending to difficulties.

Additionally, the aide dives into the test of tending to potential correspondence boundaries. Maturing guardians might confront correspondence obstructions, whether because of hearing misfortune, mental changes, or different variables. The aide urges youngsters to show restraint, utilize clear and basic language, and investigate elective specialized strategies if vital. By tending to correspondence obstructions with flexibility, youngsters add to a relationship that is supported by clear and thoughtful correspondence, guaranteeing that the association stays solid.

The investigation of giving direction on critical thinking and compromise consolidates the idea of tending to likely contrasts in viewpoints and needs. Kids and their maturing guardians might have alternate points of view and needs, and the aide perceives the significance of tending to these distinctions with deference and understanding.

Youngsters are urged to take part in open discussions about their folks' inclinations, wants, and needs, establishing a climate where contrasts are recognized and regarded. By exploring contrasts with compassion, kids add to a relationship that is described by common comprehension and a common obligation to finding arrangements that oblige different points of view.

Significant to the conversation is the investigation of the likely effect of keeping a funny bone and levity. While providing care might include serious and testing minutes, the aide recommends that keeping a comical inclination can be an important strategy for dealing with especially difficult times. Kids are urged to track down snapshots of euphoria, chuckling, and gentility in the providing care venture, encouraging a positive and strong climate. By integrating humor into the providing care insight, youngsters add to a relationship that is portrayed by an equilibrium between reality and merriment, establishing a strong and elevating climate.

In addition, the aide digs into the test of tending to possible sensations of burnout or fatigue. Providing care liabilities might be sincerely requesting, and kids might encounter sensations of burnout or fatigue. The aide perceives the significance of taking care of oneself, defining limits, and looking for reprieve when required. By focusing on their own prosperity, kids add to a relationship that is supported by their profound flexibility and the ability to furnish care with sympathy.

The investigation of giving direction on critical thinking and compromise integrates the idea of encouraging a culture of consistent learning. The providing care venture is innately unique, and difficulties might advance over the long haul. The aide proposes that youngsters embrace a mentality of constant picking up, looking for information, assets, and guidance to improve their critical thinking abilities. By cultivating a culture of consistent learning, youngsters add to a relationship that is portrayed by flexibility and a proactive way to deal with tending to new difficulties.

Significant to the conversation is the investigation of the expected effect of looking for criticism and contribution from maturing guardians. The aide urges youngsters to effectively look for criticism and contribution from their folks in regards to providing care systems, inclinations, and possible changes. By including guardians in the dynamic cycle, youngsters add to a relationship that is described by shared direction and a cooperative way to deal with tending to difficulties.

Also, the aide dives into the test of tending to possible social or generational contrasts in critical thinking draws near. Social and generational variables might impact mentalities towards critical thinking and compromise. The aide urges kids to move toward these distinctions with interest, liberality, and an eagerness to figure out their folks' points of view. By exploring social and generational subtleties with deference, kids add to a relationship that is described by social responsiveness and a common appreciation for different points of view.

The investigation of giving direction on critical thinking and compromise integrates the idea of investigating imaginative and creative arrangements. A few difficulties might profit from inventive and out-of-the-crate thinking, and the aide recommends that youngsters investigate imaginative arrangements that address the exceptional necessities and inclinations of their folks. By embracing imagination, youngsters add to a relationship that is portrayed by a dynamic and innovative way to deal with critical thinking, guaranteeing that arrangements are custom fitted to the particular conditions of their maturing guardians.

Significant to the conversation is the investigation of the expected effect of recognizing and commending victories, regardless of how little. The aide urges kids to recognize and commend the triumphs and positive minutes in the providing care venture. By perceiving accomplishments, both of all shapes and sizes, kids add to a relationship that is described by a feeling of achievement and shared happiness, establishing a good and inspiring providing care climate.

Additionally, the aide digs into the test of tending to expected sensations of responsibility or deficiency in critical thinking. Kids might encounter sensations of responsibility or deficiency, particularly on the off chance that they see that they are not doing what's necessary for their maturing guardians. The aide perceives the significance of self-sympathy and urges kids to recognize and address these sentiments with help from companions, family, or experts. By exploring sensations of responsibility with understanding and self-sympathy, kids add to a relationship that is supported by their own profound prosperity.

6.3 Encouraging resilience and patience in children

In the merciful aide, "Together Through Time: A Kids' Manual for Treasuring Maturing Guardians," the part on "Empowering Strength and Persistence in Youngsters" unfurls as a piercing investigation of the excellencies that assume a critical part in exploring the intricacies of really focusing on maturing guardians. This portion digs into the meaning of versatility and persistence, offering kids significant bits of knowledge and commonsense systems to develop these characteristics as they set out on the providing care venture. By encouraging flexibility and persistence, youngsters add to a relationship that is portrayed by strength, versatility, and an unfaltering obligation to the prosperity of their maturing guardians.

The investigation starts with an affirmation of the inborn difficulties and vulnerabilities that go with the providing care venture. Really focusing on maturing guardians is a dynamic and developing cycle, frequently set apart by unanticipated difficulties and moving conditions. The aide underlines the significance of imparting versatility and persistence in kids, perceiving these characteristics as fundamental apparatuses for exploring the recurring pattern of providing care liabilities.

By encouraging an outlook that embraces difficulties as any open doors for development, youngsters establish the groundwork for a providing care venture described by versatility and determination.

Besides, the aide digs into the idea of strength as an essential quality despite difficulty. Strength includes the ability to quickly return from difficulties, misfortunes, and troublesome conditions. The aide urges kids to see difficulties not as unconquerable impediments but rather as any open doors to learn, adjust, and develop. By ingraining versatility, youngsters add to a relationship that is invigorated by the solidarity to deal with difficulties directly, cultivating a climate where the two they and their maturing guardians can explore the intricacies of maturing with beauty and assurance.

Significant to the conversation of flexibility is the investigation of building an encouraging group of people. Flexibility is in many cases sustained within the sight of steady connections, and the aide proposes that youngsters effectively search out and draw in with encouraging groups of people. This might incorporate companions, family, support gatherings, or expert assets. By cultivating an organization of help, kids add to a relationship that is described by shared encounters, direction, and an aggregate versatility that reinforces the two guardians and maturing guardians.

Besides, the aide underscores the significance of keeping a positive outlook. Energy fills in as a strong power in building flexibility, permitting youngsters to move toward difficulties with hopefulness and a confidence in their capacity to conquer impediments. The aide urges youngsters to develop a positive outlook by zeroing in on the qualities and delights inside the providing care venture. By keeping an inspirational perspective, kids add to a relationship that is portrayed by an elevating and confident climate, cultivating a climate where the two guardians and maturing guardians can track down strength in snapshots of trouble.

Urgent to the conversation is the investigation of taking care of oneself as a necessary part of strength. Really focusing on maturing guardians can be genuinely and actually requesting, and the aide perceives the significance of focusing on one's own prosperity. Youngsters are urged to take part in taking care of oneself practices that recharge their energy, whether through work out, unwinding procedures, leisure activities, or looking for proficient help when required. By focusing on taking care of oneself, youngsters add to a relationship that is supported by their own profound and actual flexibility, guaranteeing that they can keep on furnishing care with sympathy and essentialness.

The investigation of versatility integrates the idea of adjusting to change. Change is an intrinsic part of the providing care venture, and the aide recommends that youngsters approach change with adaptability and a readiness to adjust. By embracing change as a characteristic piece of the providing care process, youngsters add to a relationship that is described by a capacity to explore developing conditions with strength and a pro-active outlook.

Besides, the aide digs into the idea of tolerance as an excellence that supplements strength. Persistence includes the capacity to keep quiet and made in the face out of difficulties, vulnerabilities, and the steady idea of maturing. The aide urges youngsters to develop persistence by recognizing that the providing care venture is a long distance race as opposed to a run. By understanding that progress might require some investment, youngsters add to a relationship that is portrayed by a patient and undaunted obligation to the prosperity of their maturing guardians.

Urgent to the conversation of persistence is the investigation of setting sensible assumptions. Tolerance is many times tried when assumptions are ridiculous or unreachable. The aide recommends that youngsters lay out clear and reachable objectives in providing care, perceiving the gradual idea of progress. By setting practical assumptions, kids add to a relationship that is described by a patient and logical way to deal with the providing care venture, guaranteeing that the two guardians and maturing guardians can explore difficulties with a feeling of consistent advancement.

The investigation of tolerance integrates the idea of care. Care includes being available in the ongoing second, tolerating it without judgment. The aide urges youngsters to rehearse care in their providing care jobs, permitting them to move toward difficulties with a quiet and focused mentality. By integrating care, kids add to a relationship that is portrayed by a patient and centered presence, cultivating a climate where the two guardians and maturing guardians can explore the intricacies of maturing with a feeling of grounded mindfulness.

Besides, the aide underscores the significance of powerful correspondence as a device for building tolerance. Clear and open correspondence guarantees that all gatherings engaged with providing care are in total agreement, diminishing false impressions and possible wellsprings of dissatisfaction. The aide urges kids to discuss transparently with their maturing guardians, kin, and other involved parties. By cultivating powerful correspondence, kids add to a relationship that is described by a patient and cooperative way to deal with critical thinking and independent direction.

Urgent to the conversation is the investigation of appreciation as a training that upgrades persistence. Appreciation includes perceiving and valuing the positive parts of the providing care venture. The aide recommends that kids develop appreciation by thinking about the significant minutes, delights, and positive commitments inside their providing care jobs. By rehearsing appreciation, kids add to a relationship that is portrayed by a patient and grateful point of view, cultivating a climate where the two guardians and maturing guardians can track down satisfaction amidst challenges.

The investigation of tolerance integrates the idea of limit setting. Limits are fundamental for keeping a good arrangement in providing care, and the aide urges kids to lay out clear limits that focus on their prosperity. By defining limits, youngsters add to a relationship that is described by a patient and reasonable way to deal with providing care, guaranteeing that they can furnish care with a feeling of equilibrium and individual satisfaction.

Also, the aide dives into the test of tending to expected sensations of culpability or deficiency. Kids might encounter sensations of responsibility, particularly in the event that they see that they are not measuring up to their own assumptions or those of their maturing guardians. The aide perceives the significance of self-empathy and urges youngsters to recognize and address these sentiments with help from companions, family, or experts. By exploring sensations of culpability with understanding and self-sympathy, youngsters add to a relationship that is supported by their own close to home prosperity.

Critical to the conversation is the investigation of the likely effect of looking for outer help. Persistence might be tried when difficulties become especially requesting, and the aide proposes that kids investigate the choice of looking for outside help when required. This might include drawing in with help gatherings, looking for direction from experts, or getting to local area assets. By perceiving the worth of outside help, kids add to a relationship that is portrayed by a patient and cooperative way to deal with providing care, guaranteeing that the providing care venture is shared and manageable.

Additionally, the aide digs into the test of tending to expected clashes or conflicts inside the family. Tolerance is much of the time expected in exploring varying viewpoints, and the aide perceives the significance of tending to clashes with sympathy and open correspondence. By encouraging a culture of understanding and split the difference, kids add to a relationship that is strong even with difficulties and portrayed by a patient and cooperative obligation to the prosperity of their maturing guardians.

The investigation of empowering strength and tolerance in youngsters fills in as a humane and viable aide inside the excursion of loving maturing guardians. By ingraining these ideals, kids add to a relationship that is portrayed by strength, flexibility, and a relentless obligation to exploring the intricacies of maturing with effortlessness and sympathy. This investigation highlights that reassuring versatility and persistence isn't just a fundamental part of providing care yet a groundbreaking chance to cultivate getting through securities, sustain close to home prosperity, and move toward the providing care venture with a heart loaded with sympathy and enduring commitment.

# Chapter 7

Balancing Responsibilities

In the genuine aide, "Together Through Time: A Youngsters' Manual for Esteeming Maturing Guardians," the section on "Adjusting Liabilities" unfurls as a significant investigation of the complicated dance between providing care obligations and the bunch liabilities that kids might shuffle in their lives. This section dives into the intricacies of adjusting proficient, individual, and providing care jobs, offering kids significant experiences and reasonable systems to explore the fragile harmony required. By excelling at adjusting liabilities, youngsters add to a relationship with their maturing guardians that is described by concordance, supportability, and a common obligation to the prosperity of all included.

The investigation starts with an affirmation of the multi-layered nature of kids' lives. Numerous kids, as they take on providing care liabilities, may likewise be adjusting vocations, individual connections, and their own prosperity. The aide underlines that perceiving the different jobs and obligations in a youngster's life is urgent for fostering a fair way to deal with providing care. By recognizing the interconnectedness of these obligations, kids can approach providing care with a comprehensive mentality, guaranteeing that every part of their lives is thought of and tended to with care.

Besides, the aide digs into the idea of laying out boundaries. Adjusting liabilities requires a smart way to deal with prioritization, and the aide proposes that youngsters ponder their needs in providing care, work, and individual life. By laying out clear needs, kids add to a relationship that is described by an engaged and deliberate distribution of significant investment. Defining boundaries permits kids to explore the intricacies of providing care with a feeling of motivation, guaranteeing that the prosperity of their maturing guardians is at the front of their contemplations.

Critical to the conversation of adjusting liabilities is the investigation of powerful using time productively. Time is a valuable asset, and the aide urges kids to foster successful time usage abilities to explore the requests of providing care, work, and individual life. By embracing systems, for example, making plans, focusing on errands, and streamlining efficiency, youngsters add to a relationship that is described by a reasonable and proficient way to deal with satisfying their different obligations. Powerful using time effectively guarantees that every part of their lives gets the consideration it merits, encouraging a climate where providing care can coincide amicably with different obligations.

Also, the aide underlines the significance of setting practical assumptions. Adjusting liabilities requires a comprehension of one's impediments and the acknowledgment that specific errands might take more time or require more exertion. The aide recommends that youngsters lay out practical assumptions for themselves in providing care, work, and individual life. By embracing sensible assumptions, kids add to a relationship that is portrayed by a fair and feasible way to deal with providing care, relieving the potential for burnout or deep-seated insecurities.

Urgent to the conversation of adjusting liabilities is the investigation of the expected effect of adaptable work courses of action. Numerous kids might be shuffling providing care liabilities with their expert jobs, and the aide perceives the significance of investigating adaptable work choices. Whether through remote work, adaptable hours, or different facilities, youngsters can look for plans that line up with their providing care obligations. By supporting for adaptability, youngsters add to a relationship that is portrayed by an amicable mixing of expert and providing care liabilities, guaranteeing that the two parts of their lives can be obliged really.

Additionally, the aide digs into the idea of successful correspondence with businesses and associates. Open openness is of the utmost importance while offsetting providing care liabilities with work commitments, and the aide urges youngsters to have straightforward conversations with their managers and partners. By encouraging comprehension and coordinated effort in the working environment, youngsters add to a relationship that is portrayed by a steady and obliging proficient climate. Powerful correspondence guarantees that youngsters can explore the requests of work while satisfying their providing care obligations capably.

The investigation of adjusting liabilities integrates the idea of taking care of oneself. Adjusting numerous obligations can be requesting, and the aide perceives the significance of focusing on one's own prosperity. Kids are urged to take part in taking care of oneself practices that recharge their energy, whether through work out, unwinding procedures, leisure activities, or looking for proficient help when required. By focusing on taking care of oneself, youngsters add to a relationship that is portrayed by their own profound and actual prosperity, guaranteeing that they can approach providing care and different obligations with strength and imperativeness.

Pivotal to the conversation is the investigation of the expected effect of including other relatives in providing care liabilities. Adjusting liabilities turns out to be more practical when providing care is a common undertaking, and the aide recommends that youngsters investigate ways of including other relatives in providing care errands. By cultivating a co-operative methodology inside the family, youngsters add to a relationship that is portrayed by shared liabilities and common help. Including other relatives makes an organization of care that eases up the singular weight, advancing an amicable harmony among providing care and different obligations.

Additionally, the aide digs into the test of tending to possible sensations of culpability or deficiency. Adjusting liabilities might bring out sensations of responsibility, particularly in the event that youngsters see that they are not living up to their own assumptions or those of their maturing guardians. The aide perceives the significance of self-sympathy and urges youngsters to recognize and address these sentiments with help from companions, family, or experts. By exploring sensations of culpability with understanding and self-empathy, youngsters add to a relationship that is supported by their own close to home prosperity.

The investigation of adjusting liabilities integrates the idea of looking for outside help. Adjusting various obligations might need outside help, and the aide recommends that kids investigate accessible encouraging groups of people, local area assets, or expert help. By looking for outer help, kids add to a relationship that is reinforced by an organization of care and help, guaranteeing that the providing care venture is shared and practical.

Urgent to the conversation is the investigation of the likely effect of defining limits. Adjusting liabilities requires laying out clear limits to forestall burnout and keep a good overall arrangement between providing care, work, and individual life. The aide urges youngsters to define limits that focus on their prosperity and forestall the obscuring of lines among expert and individual obligations. By laying out limits, kids add to a relationship that is portrayed by a reasonable and supportable way to deal with providing care, guaranteeing that they can give care a feeling of balance.

Also, the aide digs into the test of tending to likely contentions or conflicts inside the family. Adjusting liabilities might lead to clashes, and the aide perceives the significance of resolving these issues with compassion and open correspondence. By encouraging a culture of understanding and split the difference, kids add to a relationship that is strong notwithstanding challenges and described by a fair and cooperative obligation to the prosperity of their maturing guardians.

The investigation of adjusting liabilities integrates the idea of intermittently reconsidering needs and systems. The requests of providing care, work, and individual life might advance, and the aide recommends that youngsters occasionally reconsider their needs and methodologies for adjusting liabilities. By embracing an adaptable and versatile methodology, youngsters add to a relationship that is described by a continuous and dynamic reaction to the changing idea of providing care and different obligations.

Pivotal to the conversation is the investigation of the possible effect of recognizing individual restrictions. Adjusting liabilities requires one's very own affirmation limits and the acknowledgment that looking for help or designating errands is an indication of solidarity, not shortcoming. The aide urges kids to perceive when they need help and to connect for help when essential. By recognizing individual impediments, youngsters add to a relationship that is portrayed by modesty and a reasonable comprehension of their ability to offset providing care with different obligations.

Besides, the aide dives into the test of tending to expected sensations of burnout or fatigue. Adjusting various obligations might be genuinely and actually requesting, and the aide perceives the significance of taking care of oneself, defining limits, and looking for reprieve when required. By focusing on their own prosperity, youngsters add to a relationship that is supported by their close to home versatility and the ability to furnish care with sympathy.

7.1 Exploring the importance of balance in children's lives

In the wise aide, "Together Through Time: A Kids' Manual for Treasuring Maturing Guardians," the section on "Investigating the Significance of Equilibrium in Youngsters' Lives" unfurls as a smart assessment of the basic job that equilibrium plays in the existences of kids who are exploring the obligations of providing care for maturing guardians. This section digs into the diverse elements of equilibrium, investigating its importance with regards to providing care as well as in the more extensive range of kids' lives. By getting it and embracing balance, kids can encourage a comprehensive way to deal with their jobs, guaranteeing that they take care of providing care liabilities while keeping up with harmony in their own, proficient, and close to home circles.

The investigation starts with an affirmation of the different jobs that youngsters frequently play in their lives. Past the providing care liabilities, youngsters might be understudies, experts, accomplices, guardians, and people with individual goals and responsibilities. The aide stresses that perceiving and esteeming the different features of a youngster's character is pivotal for accomplishing a feeling of equilibrium. By valuing the interconnectedness of these jobs, youngsters can approach providing care with a thorough comprehension of how it coordinates into the more extensive embroidery of their lives.

Besides, the aide dives into the idea of equilibrium as a dynamic and steadily developing cycle. Adjusting numerous jobs requires an adaptable and versatile mentality, perceiving that needs and conditions might move after some time. The aide proposes that kids embrace a liquid way to deal with balance, recognizing that changes and recalibrations are normal parts of overseeing different obligations. By developing flexibility, youngsters add to a relationship with their maturing guardians that is described by versatility and responsiveness to the changing elements of providing care.

Vital to the conversation of equilibrium is the investigation of the significance of mindfulness. Grasping one's own requirements, impediments, and yearnings is fundamental to accomplishing balance in different life spaces. The aide urges youngsters to take part in self-reflection, encouraging a consciousness of their physical, close to home, and mental prosperity. By developing mindfulness, kids add to a relationship that is portrayed by a fair and careful way to deal with providing care, guaranteeing that their own requirements are thought of and tended to inside the providing care venture.

In addition, the aide stresses the job of viable time usage in accomplishing balance. Time is a limited asset, and the aide proposes that kids foster abilities in using time productively to streamline their timetables. By focusing on errands, defining sensible objectives, and laying out productive work processes, kids add to a relationship that is described by a decent and deliberate distribution of time to providing care, work, special goals, and taking care of oneself. Powerful time usage fills in as a device for exploring the requests of different obligations without feeling overpowered or extended excessively meager.

Significant to the conversation of equilibrium is the investigation of defining limits. Laying out clear limits is fundamental for keeping a sound balance between providing care, work, individual life, and taking care of oneself. The aide urges kids to characterize their cutoff points, impart them really, and regard their own requirement for balance. By defining limits, kids add to a relationship that is portrayed by a fair and manageable way to deal with providing care, guaranteeing that they can satisfy their obligations without undermining their prosperity.

Besides, the aide dives into the idea of comprehensive prosperity. Balance reaches out past the circulation of significant investment; it envelops the general prosperity of the youngster. The aide proposes that kids focus on their physical, profound, and psychological wellness as essential parts of accomplishing balance. By embracing all encompassing prosperity, youngsters add to a relationship that is described by a reasonable and dynamic way to deal with providing care, guaranteeing that they can furnish care with imperativeness and strength.

Significant to the conversation is the investigation of the possible effect of keeping up with open correspondence. Balance is cultivated through straightforward correspondence with maturing guardians, relatives, and different partners. The aide urges youngsters to convey straightforwardly about their responsibilities, difficulties, and necessities. By encouraging a culture of open correspondence, youngsters add to a relationship that is described by a reasonable and cooperative way to deal with providing care. Viable correspondence guarantees that all elaborate gatherings know about one another's assumptions, cultivating a climate where providing care liabilities can be shared and adjusted really.

Also, the aide underscores the significance of setting reasonable assumptions for oneself. Unreasonable assumptions can prompt insecurities and stress. The aide proposes that kids lay out clear and feasible objectives, perceiving that equilibrium requires a sober minded and estimated approach. By setting sensible assumptions, kids add to a relationship that is portrayed by a decent and practical way to deal with providing care, guaranteeing that they can meet their obligations without encountering unjustifiable strain.

The investigation of equilibrium consolidates the idea of encouraging an encouraging group of people. Building an organization of help is instrumental in accomplishing balance, and the aide urges kids to draw in with companions, family, support gatherings, or expert assets. By encouraging an encouraging group of people, kids add to a relationship that is described by shared encounters, direction, and an aggregate strength that reinforces the two guardians and maturing guardians. In the midst of challenge or when equilibrium becomes tricky, the encouraging group of people fills in as a wellspring of solidarity and consolation.

Vital to the conversation is the investigation of the possible effect of taking care of oneself practices. Adjusting liabilities requires an interest in one's own prosperity, and the aide recommends that kids take part in taking care of oneself practices that renew their energy and encourage a feeling of equilibrium. Whether through work out, unwinding strategies, leisure activities, or looking for proficient help when required, taking care of oneself assumes a vital part in keeping up with balance. By focusing on taking care of oneself, kids add to a relationship that is described by their own close to home and actual prosperity, guaranteeing that they can approach providing care and different obligations with strength and imperativeness.

In addition, the aide dives into the test of tending to possible sensations of culpability or deficiency. Youngsters might encounter sensations of culpability, particularly on the off chance that they see that they are not measuring up to their own assumptions or those of their maturing guardians. The aide perceives the significance of self-empathy and urges youngsters to recognize and address these sentiments with help from companions, family, or experts. By exploring sensations of culpability with understanding and self-empathy, kids add to a relationship that is supported by their own profound prosperity.

The investigation of equilibrium integrates the idea of intermittent reassessment and change. Accomplishing and keeping up with balance is a continuous cycle that requires intermittent reassessment of needs, procedures, and prosperity. The aide recommends that youngsters intermittently consider their responsibilities and change their ways to deal with balance in light of advancing conditions. By taking on a proactive and intelligent position, kids add to a relationship that is portrayed by a dynamic and responsive way to deal with the difficulties and delights of providing care.

Significant to the conversation is the investigation of the possible effect of embracing defect. Adjusting liabilities frequently includes exploring vulnerabilities and adjusting to unexpected difficulties. The aide urges youngsters to embrace defect, perceiving that equilibrium isn't tied in with accomplishing flawlessness however about tracking down amicability in the midst of the intricacies of life. By developing a mentality that acknowledges blemishes and gains from difficulties, kids add to a relationship that is portrayed by strength and a capacity to explore the capricious idea of providing care with effortlessness and understanding.

In addition, the aide dives into the test of tending to expected clashes or conflicts inside the family. Adjusting liabilities might bring about clashes, and the aide perceives the significance of resolving these issues with sympathy and open correspondence. By encouraging a culture of understanding and split the difference, youngsters add to a relationship that is versatile even with difficulties and portrayed by a reasonable and cooperative obligation to the prosperity of their maturing guardians.

7.2 Offering strategies for managing caregiving responsibilities alongside other commitments

In the sympathetic aide, "Together Through Time: A Youngsters' Manual for Treasuring Maturing Guardians," this portion centers around offering methodologies for overseeing providing care liabilities close by different responsibilities. Adjusting the perplexing requests of providing care with different features of life requires smart preparation, powerful using time effectively, and an all encompassing methodology.

By carrying out viable techniques, youngsters can explore the intricacies of providing care while keeping up with balance in their own, proficient, and profound circles.

The investigation starts with an accentuation on the significance of compelling using time effectively. Perceiving that time is a limited asset, youngsters are urged to foster abilities that improve their timetables. Methodologies, for example, making day to day or week after week designs, focusing on undertakings, and utilizing efficiency apparatuses can support dispensing time proficiently. By embracing powerful time usage rehearses, youngsters add to a relationship that is described by a reasonable and deliberate dispersion of time across providing care, work, special goals, and taking care of oneself.

Also, the aide digs into the idea of defining boundaries. To oversee providing care liabilities close by different responsibilities, youngsters are urged to lay out clear needs. This includes recognizing the most basic errands and dispensing investment in like manner. By adjusting needs to general objectives, youngsters add to a relationship that is described by an engaged and purposeful way to deal with providing care, guaranteeing that their endeavors line up with the prosperity of their maturing guardians and different obligations.

Essential to the conversation of overseeing providing care liabilities is the investigation of adaptable work game plans. Numerous kids might be shuffling proficient jobs close by providing care, and investigating adaptable work choices can fundamentally facilitate this difficult exercise. Remote work, adaptable hours, or different facilities can give the essential adaptability to satisfy providing care obligations while meeting proficient responsibilities. By supporting for and arranging adaptable work plans, kids add to a relationship that is described by an amicable mixing of expert and providing care liabilities.

Additionally, the aide underscores the job of viable correspondence in overseeing providing care liabilities. Open and straightforward correspondence with managers, partners, and relatives is instrumental in accomplishing a harmony among providing care and different responsibilities. Youngsters are urged to impart proactively about their obligations, set sensible assumptions, and look for help when required. By encouraging comprehension and joint effort through compelling correspondence, kids add to a relationship that is described by a reasonable and cooperative way to deal with providing care.

Urgent to the conversation of overseeing providing care liabilities is the investigation of including other relatives. Shared providing care liabilities appropriate the responsibility and offer close to home help. Kids are urged to draw in with kin, family members, or other relatives to make a cooperative providing care organization. By including other relatives, youngsters add to a relationship that is described by shared liabilities and common help, cultivating a feeling of solidarity and collaboration in focusing on maturing guardians.

Also, the aide dives into the idea of utilizing local area assets. Neighborhood associations, support gatherings, or local area administrations can offer significant help with overseeing providing care liabilities. Youngsters are urged to investigate accessible assets that can give relief, direction, or extra help. By taking advantage of local area assets, youngsters add to a relationship that is portrayed by an organization of care past the nuclear family, improving the providing care insight and upgrading their capacity to adjust liabilities.

Critical to the conversation of overseeing providing care liabilities is the investigation of the expected effect of taking care of oneself practices. Focusing on taking care of oneself is fundamental for keeping up with physical, profound, and mental prosperity. Youngsters are urged to participate in taking care of oneself exercises that re-energize their energy and mitigate pressure. Whether through work out, contemplation, side interests, or looking for proficient help, taking care of oneself is a crucial procedure for dealing with the requests of providing care close by different responsibilities. By focusing on taking care of oneself, kids add to a relationship that is portrayed by their own close to home flexibility and the ability to furnish care with empathy.

Also, the aide stresses the significance of setting sensible assumptions for oneself. Unreasonable assumptions can prompt pressure and insecurities. Youngsters are urged to lay out clear and reachable objectives, perceiving that equilibrium requires a sober minded and estimated approach. By setting reasonable assumptions, kids add to a relationship that is portrayed by a fair and feasible way to deal with providing care, guaranteeing that they can meet their obligations without encountering excessive strain.

The investigation of overseeing providing care liabilities consolidates the idea of compelling appointment. Youngsters are urged to appoint errands when fitting, whether inside the family or through proficient administrations. Assigning liabilities can ease up the responsibility, giving youngsters the vital space to satisfy their providing care obligations while overseeing different responsibilities. By excelling at designation, youngsters add to a relationship that is portrayed by a decent and shared way to deal with providing care, guaranteeing that errands are circulated effectively.

Essential to the conversation is the investigation of occasional re-assessment and change. Adjusting providing care liabilities requires a continuous assessment of needs, systems, and prosperity. Kids are urged to occasionally rethink their responsibilities and make changes in light of advancing conditions. By embracing a proactive and intelligent position, kids add to a relationship that is portrayed by a dynamic and responsive way to deal with the difficulties and delights of providing care.

Additionally, the aide digs into the test of tending to possible sensations of culpability or deficiency. Youngsters might encounter sensations of responsibility, particularly on the off chance that they see that they are not living up to their own assumptions or those of their maturing guardians. The aide perceives the significance of self-sympathy and urges youngsters to recognize and address these sentiments with help from companions, family, or experts. By exploring sensations of culpability with understanding and self-sympathy, youngsters add to a relationship that is supported by their own profound prosperity.

The investigation of overseeing providing care liabilities integrates the idea of encouraging open correspondence inside the family. Clear correspondence about jobs, assumptions, and potential difficulties is fundamental for a decent providing care dynamic. Kids are urged to participate in standard family conversations to guarantee that everybody is in total agreement and that obligations are shared really. By encouraging a culture of open correspondence, kids add to a relationship that is described by a decent and cooperative way to deal with providing care.

Pivotal to the conversation is the investigation of the expected effect of including maturing guardians in navigation. Including maturing guardians in conversations about their consideration inclinations, necessities, and choices enables them and encourages a cooperative way to deal with providing care. Youngsters are urged to participate in open and conscious discourse with their maturing guardians, looking for their feedback and including them in choices about their consideration. By integrating maturing guardians into the dynamic cycle, youngsters add to a relationship that is portrayed by shared liability and a decent way to deal with providing care.

In addition, the aide dives into the test of tending to likely struggles or conflicts inside the family. Adjusting providing care liabilities might bring about clashes, and the aide perceives the significance of resolving these issues with sympathy and open correspondence. By encouraging a culture of understanding and split the difference, kids add to a relationship that is strong notwithstanding challenges and described by a reasonable and cooperative obligation to the prosperity of their maturing guardians.

7.3 Emphasizing the significance of self-care for children

Inside the compassionate aide, "Together Through Time: A Youngsters' Manual for Loving Maturing Guardians," this segment underscores the significant meaning of taking care of oneself for kids. Really focusing on maturing guardians can be genuinely and truly requesting, and focusing on one's own prosperity isn't just a pragmatic need however a groundbreaking demonstration of empathy. By digging into the significance of taking care of oneself, kids can develop strength, keep up with profound harmony, and move toward the intricacies of providing care with a supported and sympathetic heart.

The investigation starts by featuring the interconnectedness of taking care of oneself and compelling providing care. Perceiving that providing care is a requesting liability, the aide highlights that taking care of oneself isn't an extravagance however a fundamental starting point for giving supported and sympathetic consideration. Youngsters are urged to see taking care of oneself not as a self centered try but rather as an essential for satisfying their providing care jobs with imperativeness and profound strength. By focusing on taking care of oneself, youngsters add to a relationship that is portrayed by their own prosperity, guaranteeing that they can explore the difficulties of providing care with strength and empathy.

Additionally, the aide dives into the diverse components of taking care of oneself, including physical, close to home, and mental prosperity. Actual taking care of oneself includes sustaining the body through sufficient rest, nourishment, and exercise. Youngsters are urged to focus on their actual wellbeing, perceiving that a very much supported and rested body is better prepared to deal with the requests of providing care. By embracing actual taking care of oneself, youngsters add to a relationship that is described by their own imperativeness, guaranteeing that they approach providing care with a hearty and stimulated presence.

Urgent to the conversation is the investigation of profound taking care of oneself. Really focusing on maturing guardians might inspire a scope of feelings, from affection and satisfaction to stress and misery. The aide urges kids to recognize and deal with their feelings, looking for help from companions, family, or experts when required. By embracing close to home taking care of oneself, youngsters add to a relationship that is portrayed by their own profound strength, guaranteeing that they can explore the profound intricacies of providing care with sympathy and understanding.

Besides, the aide accentuates the job of mental taking care of oneself in keeping up with mental prosperity. Offsetting providing care liabilities with different responsibilities might be intellectually burdening, and youngsters are urged to participate in exercises that animate their psyches and give mental restoration. Whether through side interests, learning open doors, or unwinding procedures, mental taking care of oneself is an essential part of supporting mental wellbeing. By focusing on mental taking care of oneself, kids add to a relationship that is portrayed by a fair and clear-disapproved of way to deal with providing care, guaranteeing that they can settle on informed choices and explore difficulties with smartness.

Essential to the conversation of taking care of oneself is the investigation of the likely effect of defining limits. Laying out clear limits is fundamental for safeguarding one's prosperity and forestalling burnout. The aide urges kids to characterize their cutoff points, convey them actually, and regard their own requirement for balance. By defining limits, kids add to a relationship that is portrayed by a reasonable and practical way to deal with providing care, guaranteeing that they can give care a feeling of balance.

Also, the aide digs into the test of tending to expected sensations of culpability or deficiency related with setting aside some margin for taking care of oneself. Youngsters might encounter responsibility, particularly assuming they see that they are dismissing their providing care obligations. The aide perceives the significance of self-sympathy and urges youngsters to recognize and address these sentiments with understanding. By exploring sensations of culpability with self-sympathy, youngsters add to a relationship that is supported by their own close to home prosperity.

The investigation of taking care of oneself integrates the idea of occasional reassessment and change. Taking care of oneself is certainly not a static undertaking however a unique cycle that requires intermittent reflection and changes. The aide recommends that kids occasionally reconsider their taking care of oneself schedules in view of advancing conditions. By embracing a proactive and intelligent position, youngsters add to a relationship that is portrayed by a dynamic and responsive way to deal with their own prosperity inside the providing care venture.

Critical to the conversation is the investigation of the expected effect of looking for outer help. Taking care of oneself might include connecting for help when required, whether through companions, family, or expert administrations. The aide perceives the worth of outside help in upgrading taking care of oneself practices. By recognizing the significance of looking for outside help, youngsters add to a relationship that is described by an organization of care, guaranteeing that they have the assets and help important to focus on their own prosperity.

In addition, the aide dives into the test of adjusting taking care of oneself with providing care liabilities. Youngsters might wrestle with the discernment that setting aside margin for themselves is inconsistent with satisfying their providing care jobs. The aide challenges this thought, stressing that taking care of oneself isn't an interruption from providing care yet a basic piece of giving reasonable and humane consideration. By perceiving the similarity of taking care of oneself and providing care, kids add to a relationship that is described by an all encompassing and adjusted way to deal with the obligations of really focusing on maturing guardians.

The investigation of taking care of oneself consolidates the idea of cultivating open correspondence inside the family. Clear correspondence about the significance of taking care of oneself is essential for establishing a steady climate. Youngsters are urged to discuss straightforwardly with relatives about their taking care of oneself requirements, assumptions, and the common comprehension that taking care of oneself is fundamental for powerful providing care. By encouraging a culture of open correspondence, youngsters add to a relationship that is portrayed by a decent and cooperative way to deal with providing care and taking care of oneself.

Vital to the conversation is the investigation of the expected effect of incorporating taking care of oneself into the providing care schedule. Taking care of oneself ought not be seen as a different substance however as a fundamental piece of the providing care venture. The aide proposes that youngsters coordinate taking care of oneself practices into their everyday schedules, guaranteeing that snapshots of revival are woven consistently into the texture of providing care. By embracing taking care of oneself as an essential part of the providing care schedule, kids add to a relationship that is portrayed by a reasonable and maintainable way to deal with really focusing on maturing guardians.

Besides, the aide dives into the test of tending to likely struggles or conflicts inside the family with respect to taking care of oneself. Relational intricacies might impact impression of taking care of oneself, and the aide perceives the significance of resolving these issues with sympathy and open correspondence. By encouraging a culture of understanding and split the difference, kids add to a relationship that is versatile even with difficulties and portrayed by a reasonable and cooperative obligation to the prosperity of their maturing guardians and themselves.

# Chapter 8

Passing Down Values

Inside the smart aide, "Together Through Time: A Youngsters' Manual for Esteeming Maturing Guardians," this section digs into the critical part of passing down values starting with one age then onto the next. The transmission of values holds significant significance in the excursion of loving maturing guardians, cultivating a feeling of progression, and molding the underpinning of familial bonds. By investigating the rich embroidery of values, youngsters can develop a profound association with their maturing guardians, add to a tradition of shared standards, and explore the intricacies of providing care with a groundwork of persevering and loved values.

The investigation starts by perceiving the intrinsic job values play in forming familial character. Values act as core values that illuminate ways of behaving, choices, and the general culture inside a family. Youngsters are urged to consider the qualities imparted by their folks and to perceive the meaning of these standards in shaping the family's character. By recognizing the job of values, youngsters add to a relationship that is described by a mutual perspective of the center rules that have formed and keep on impacting the family.

Additionally, the aide digs into the idea of open correspondence about values. Significant discussions about values make a stage for understanding and valuing the viewpoints of maturing guardians. Youngsters are urged to participate in open and deferential discoursed about the qualities that hold importance for their folks, investigating the encounters and life illustrations that have molded these standards. By encouraging open correspondence about values, youngsters add to a relationship that is described by shared understanding and an appreciation for the different points of view that improve the family's aggregate personality.

Significant to the conversation is the investigation of the likely effect of safeguarding social and familial customs. Many qualities are implanted in social and familial customs that are gone down through ages. The aide perceives the significance of saving and commending these practices for of communicating values. Kids are urged to take part in and proceed with customs that hold extraordinary importance for their maturing guardians effectively. By safeguarding social and familial practices, youngsters add to a relationship that is described by an association with shared roots and a coherence of values that have been loved across ages.

Also, the aide underscores the job of displaying values through activities. Values are imparted through words as well as are significantly impacted by activities and ways of behaving. Youngsters are urged to notice the qualities encapsulated by their maturing guardians in ordinary activities, choices, and cooperations. By displaying values through their own decisions, kids add to a relationship that is described by a lived articulation of shared standards, supporting the meaning of these qualities in the texture of the family.

Vital to the conversation of passing down values is the investigation of the expected effect of deliberate narrating. Narrating fills in as a useful asset for communicating values, permitting guardians to share their background, difficulties, wins, and the rules that directed them. The aide proposes that youngsters effectively take part in discussions that brief their maturing guardians to share tales about their qualities, convictions, and the illustrations they have advanced along their life process. By partaking in purposeful narrating, kids add to a relationship that is portrayed by a rich story of shared values, making an embroidery of understanding that fortifies the connection between ages.

In addition, the aide digs into the idea of investigating the qualities that reverberate with individual relatives. While there might be guiding principle that join the family, individual individuals may likewise hold individual qualities that add to the variety inside the familial unit. Youngsters are urged to investigate and value the exceptional qualities that reverberate with every relative, perceiving the extravagance that this variety brings to the family's aggregate personality. By recognizing and regarding individual qualities, kids add to a relationship that is described by a nuanced comprehension of the novel points of view that enhance the familial embroidery.

Urgent to the conversation of passing down values is the investigation of the expected effect of examining the meaning of values in providing care. As kids explore the obligations of really focusing on maturing guardians, the aide urges them to unequivocally talk about the qualities that guide their providing care approach. Understanding the qualities that support providing care choices makes straightforwardness and arrangement between ages. By participating in discussions about the meaning of values in providing care, kids add to a relationship that is portrayed by a common obligation to giving consideration established in the rules that make the biggest difference to the family.

In addition, the aide underscores the job of shared regard in passing down values. The transmission of values is an equal interaction that requires shared regard and understanding. Kids are urged to move toward discussions about values with receptiveness, effectively paying attention to the points of view of their maturing guardians and offering their own viewpoints with deference. By cultivating a climate of common regard, kids add to a relationship that is portrayed by an amicable trade of values, making a mutual perspective that rises above generational contrasts.

Essential to the conversation is the investigation of the expected effect of values as a wellspring of strength. Values act as a wellspring of flexibility during testing times, giving an ethical compass and a feeling of inspiration. The aide recommends that kids draw on the qualities imparted by their maturing guardians as a wellspring of solidarity and direction despite providing care difficulties. By going to shared values during troublesome minutes, youngsters add to a relationship that is portrayed by a strength established in the rules that have directed the family through ages.

Additionally, the aide digs into the idea of integrating values into direction. Values assume a significant part in molding choices, and the aide urges youngsters to purposefully integrate shared values into the dynamic cycle, particularly in regards to providing care. By adjusting choices to fundamental beliefs, youngsters add to a relationship that is described by a deliberate and principled way to deal with providing care, guaranteeing that decisions mirror the getting through rules that make the biggest difference to the family.

Essential to the conversation of passing down values is the investigation of the expected effect of considering the qualities learned through providing care encounters. Really focusing on maturing guardians offers significant examples about adoration, sympathy, tolerance, and flexibility. The aide urges kids to ponder the qualities they have learned through their providing care encounters and to perceive the groundbreaking effect of these illustrations. By pondering providing care values, youngsters add to a relationship that is described by a continuous discourse about the rules that rise out of the common excursion of really focusing on maturing guardians.

Besides, the aide stresses the job of passing down values as an inheritance. Values address a heritage that reaches out past material belongings, leaving a permanent engraving on the character of the family. Youngsters are urged to see the transmission of values as a significant heritage, perceiving the getting through influence that common standards can have on people in the future. By embracing the job of values as an inheritance, youngsters add to a relationship that is portrayed by a feeling of progression, guaranteeing that the rules that have formed the family persevere and reverberate across time.

Significant to the conversation is the investigation of the expected effect of integrating new qualities into the family story. Families advance, and the aide perceives that new qualities might arise inside the setting of evolving conditions. Kids are urged to effectively add to the family account by integrating new qualities that line up with the developing elements of the familial unit. By embracing the fuse of new qualities, kids add to a relationship that is portrayed by flexibility, guaranteeing that the family story keeps on mirroring the rules that make the biggest difference to its individuals.

In addition, the aide dives into the test of tending to possible contentions or conflicts about values inside the family. Values might lead to clashes, and the aide perceives the significance of resolving these issues with sympathy and open correspondence. By cultivating a culture of understanding and split the difference, kids add to a relationship that is versatile despite challenges and described by a reasonable and cooperative obligation to the persevering through values that characterize the family.

8.1 Discussing the legacy of love, respect, and care

Inside the sympathetic aide, "Together Through Time: A Youngsters' Manual for Esteeming Maturing Guardians," this fragment digs into a sincere conversation about the significant tradition of adoration, regard, and care inside the familial excursion. The heritage exemplifies the getting through effect of these central qualities on the familial bond, reverberating across ages and making an embroidery of association that rises above time. By investigating the tradition of affection, regard, and care, kids can extend how they might interpret the significant commitments of their maturing guardians and develop a humane way to deal with the obligations of providing care.

The investigation starts by recognizing love as the foundation of the familial heritage. Love shapes the substance of the association among guardians and youngsters, giving an establishment to trust, understanding, and everyday encouragement.

Kids are urged to consider the statements of adoration they have encountered from their maturing guardians and to perceive the immortal idea of this profound bond. By recognizing the tradition of affection, youngsters add to a relationship that is described by a profound and standing association, cultivating a comprehension that affection is a string woven through the texture of the family.

Besides, the aide digs into the idea of regard as a mainstay of the familial heritage. Regard is reflected in the shared respect, appreciation, and thought that relatives stretch out to each other. Kids are urged to think about the manners by which their maturing guardians have exhibited and imparted the worth of regard inside the family. By perceiving and regarding the tradition of regard, youngsters add to a relationship that is described by an underpinning of shared regard, establishing a climate where every relative's nobility is maintained and esteemed.

Vital to the conversation is the investigation of care as a necessary piece of the familial heritage. Care includes the arrangement of physical, close to home, and reasonable help that supports the prosperity of relatives. Youngsters are urged to consider the providing care acts they have seen from their maturing guardians and to see the value in the magnanimity and devotion implanted in these demonstrations of care. By recognizing the tradition of care, youngsters add to a relationship that is described by a culture of help and empathy, perceiving that providing care is an outflow of affection and a fundamental part of the familial heritage.

Additionally, the aide underscores the job of correspondence inside the tradition of adoration, regard, and care. Correspondence includes the common trade of these qualities, making a dynamic and interconnected relationship. Youngsters are urged to effectively partake in responding adoration, regard, and care toward their maturing guardians, perceiving that the heritage is supported through the continuous trade of these fundamental qualities. By embracing correspondence, youngsters add to a relationship that is portrayed by an amicable and adjusted progression of affection, regard, and care, guaranteeing that these qualities keep on improving the familial bond.

Significant to the conversation of the heritage is the investigation of the likely effect of displaying affection, regard, and care in providing care. As kids explore the obligations of really focusing on maturing guardians, the aide urges them to demonstrate the upsides of affection, regard, and care in their providing care approach. By exemplifying these qualities through activities, youngsters add to a relationship that is portrayed by a continuation of the heritage, guaranteeing that providing care turns into an indication of the getting through rules that have molded the family.

Additionally, the aide digs into the idea of offering thanks for the tradition of adoration, regard, and care. Appreciation fills in as a strong affirmation of the commitments made by maturing guardians in forming the familial heritage.

Youngsters are urged to offer their thanks, both verbally and through significant activities, perceiving the meaning of the heritage in molding their personality and the family's aggregate character. By offering thanks, youngsters add to a relationship that is portrayed by an affirmation of the getting through effect of adoration, regard, and care.

Vital to the conversation of the heritage is the investigation of the likely effect of passing on the upsides of adoration, regard, and care to people in the future. The aide perceives that the inheritance stretches out past the ongoing age and can possibly shape the upsides of future relatives. Youngsters are urged to effectively take part in passing on the upsides of adoration, regard, and care to their own kids, adding to a heritage that resounds across time. By becoming stewards of the inheritance, youngsters guarantee that the basic qualities persevere and keep on molding the familial bond for a long time into the future.

Also, the aide accentuates the job of reflection on the examples gained from the tradition of affection, regard, and care. The heritage offers significant illustrations about the significance of these qualities in making a strong and associated family. Youngsters are urged to think about the illustrations gained from the heritage, perceiving how love, regard, and care have added to the family's solidarity and solidarity. By taking part in intelligent practices, kids add to a relationship that is described by a continuous discourse about the persevering through illustrations implanted in the heritage.

Significant to the conversation is the investigation of the likely effect of adoration, regard, and care as wellsprings of flexibility during testing times. The inheritance fills in as a supply of solidarity during snapshots of trouble, giving an ethical compass and a wellspring of solace. The aide recommends that youngsters draw on the tradition of affection, regard, and care during providing care difficulties, perceiving the groundbreaking effect of these qualities in encouraging versatility. By going to the heritage during troublesome minutes, youngsters add to a relationship that is described by a versatility secured in the getting through rules that have directed the family.

Also, the aide digs into the idea of integrating the heritage into the providing care venture. The upsides of adoration, regard, and care are not discrete from the providing care liabilities but rather are vital to the whole excursion. Youngsters are urged to deliberately integrate the heritage into their providing care approach, guaranteeing that the standards passed down from their maturing guardians guide their choices and activities. By coordinating the inheritance into providing care, kids add to a relationship that is described by a progression of values, making a consistent association between the persevering through standards and the providing care liabilities.

Pivotal to the conversation is the investigation of the expected effect of the heritage in cultivating a feeling of solidarity and having a place inside the family. The tradition of adoration, regard, and care makes a feeling of divided personality and having a place between relatives. Kids are urged to perceive the binding together force of the inheritance, encouraging a feeling of solidarity that rises above individual contrasts. By embracing the heritage, kids add to a relationship that is portrayed by a profound feeling of association and having a place, perceiving that the qualities passed down from their maturing guardians make a bond that endures everyday hardship.

Also, the aide underscores the job of the heritage in shaping the family story. The upsides of adoration, regard, and care add to the account that characterizes the family's aggregate personality. Kids are urged to effectively take part in forming and saving the family account, perceiving the persevering through effect of the heritage on the story that is told and retold across ages. By adding to the family story, youngsters guarantee that the tradition of adoration, regard, and care turns into an essential piece of the family's personality.

Essential to the conversation is the investigation of the likely effect of the heritage in cultivating a humane way to deal with providing care. The inheritance fills in as an aide for humane providing care, mixing the obligations with a feeling of direction and commitment. Kids are urged to see providing care as an outflow of the heritage, perceiving that giving consideration is a demonstration of adoration, regard, and empathy. By adjusting providing care with the standards of the heritage, youngsters add to a relationship that is portrayed by a providing care venture injected with the immortal qualities that have formed the family.

8.2 Highlighting the values and lessons children can pass down to future generations

Inside the insightful aide, "Together Through Time: A Youngsters' Manual for Loving Maturing Guardians," this part digs into the huge job of featuring the qualities and examples that kids can pass down to people in the future. As kids explore the obligations of really focusing on maturing guardians, they become stewards of a heritage and assume a urgent part in molding the story that will reverberate with the ages to come. By investigating the qualities and examples that kids can pass down, this guide energizes an intentional reflection on the persevering through rules that add to the familial embroidery.

The investigation starts by perceiving the extraordinary force of sympathy as a worth to be passed down. Compassion includes understanding and talking about the thoughts of another, and kids are urged to develop this quality in their connections with their maturing guardians.

By sympathizing with the difficulties and delights experienced by their folks, youngsters add to a relationship that is portrayed by a profound comprehension and close to home association. Passing down sympathy turns into a significant example, showing people in the future the significance of empathy and figuring out in cultivating significant connections.

Besides, the aide underlines the job of flexibility as an illustration to be passed down to people in the future. Really focusing on maturing guardians might introduce different difficulties, and versatility is the capacity to adjust and return from hardships. Youngsters are urged to display flexibility despite providing care difficulties, showing a mentality of diligence and strength. By passing down the example of versatility, kids add to a heritage that outfits people in the future with the psychological grit to explore life's unavoidable promising and less promising times.

Pivotal to the conversation is the investigation of the possible effect of appreciation as a worth and example to be passed down. Appreciation includes perceiving and valuing the positive parts of life, even amidst difficulties. Youngsters are urged to offer thanks for the commitments of their maturing guardians, encouraging a culture of appreciation. By passing down the example of appreciation, youngsters add to a heritage that stresses the significance of perceiving and esteeming the endeavors and forfeits of the individuals who preceded.

Additionally, the aide digs into the idea of the significance of open correspondence as a worth and illustration to be passed down. Clear and legit correspondence is vital in cultivating understanding and settling clashes. Youngsters are urged to focus on open correspondence with their maturing guardians, establishing a climate where contemplations and sentiments can be communicated straightforwardly. By passing down the example of open correspondence, youngsters add to a heritage that values straightforward and conscious exchange, establishing the groundwork for solid connections in people in the future.

Vital to the conversation is the investigation of the expected effect of empathy as a worth to be passed down. Empathy includes offering grace and understanding towards others, particularly during testing times. Kids are urged to stretch out sympathy to their maturing guardians, perceiving and tending to their necessities with compassion. By passing down the worth of empathy, youngsters add to a heritage that underscores the significance of really focusing on others with a veritable and figuring out heart.

Besides, the aide stresses the job of versatility as an example to be passed down. Life is dynamic and frequently expects people to adjust to evolving conditions. Youngsters are urged to exhibit adaptability and flexibility in their providing care jobs, embracing significantly impact with a positive mentality. By passing down the example of flexibility, youngsters add to an inheritance that gets ready people in the future to explore the vulnerabilities of existence with versatility and a readiness to embrace new difficulties.

Significant to the conversation is the investigation of the likely effect of the significance of taking care of oneself as a worth and illustration to be passed down. Really focusing on maturing guardians can be genuinely and actually requesting, featuring the need of focusing on one's own prosperity. Kids are urged to display and promoter for taking care of oneself, perceiving that keeping up with individual wellbeing is essential for giving viable consideration to other people. By passing down the example of taking care of oneself, kids add to an inheritance that esteems the significance of keeping a good overall arrangement between providing care liabilities and individual prosperity.

Additionally, the aide digs into the idea of the meaning of family bonds as a worth to be passed down. Family fills in as a mainstay of help and association, and kids are urged to areas of strength for support bonds by encouraging positive associations with their maturing guardians and among kin. By passing down the worth of family bonds, kids add to an inheritance that focuses on the significance of a strong and interconnected nuclear family.

Critical to the conversation is the investigation of the possible effect of the worth of time and presence as an example to be passed down. Time is a valuable item, and kids are urged to focus on quality time with their maturing guardians. By being available and effectively took part in minutes together, kids pass down the illustration that time put resources into connections is a significant and indispensable gift. This illustration underscores the significance of appreciating minutes with friends and family and gaining significant experiences that persevere through ages.

Also, the aide underscores the job of the worth of deep rooted advancing as an example to be passed down. The excursion of really focusing on maturing guardians presents various open doors for learning and self-awareness. Youngsters are urged to move toward the providing care insight with interest and a promise to persistent learning. By passing down the example of deep rooted learning, kids add to a heritage that esteems the obtaining of information, flexibility, and the quest for self-awareness all through one's life.

Critical to the conversation is the investigation of the expected effect of the example of freedom as a worth to be passed down. Maturing guardians might appreciate their freedom, and kids are urged to regard and support their independence. By passing down the example of freedom, youngsters add to an inheritance that esteems the significance of cultivating independence and independence, permitting people in the future to mature with nobility and a feeling of command over their lives.

Also, the aide dives into the idea of the significance of giggling and satisfaction as values to be passed down. In the midst of the difficulties of providing care, finding snapshots of satisfaction and chuckling can be a wellspring of versatility and association.

Kids are urged to imbue humor and euphoria into their cooperations with maturing guardians, establishing a climate that elevates spirits. By passing down the upsides of chuckling and bliss, kids add to an inheritance that perceives the mending force of energy and shared snapshots of joy.

Vital to the conversation is the investigation of the expected effect of the illustration of pardoning and compromise as a worth to be passed down. Relational peculiarities might include clashes and misconceptions, and youngsters are urged to focus on absolution and compromise. By passing down the example of pardoning, kids add to a heritage that esteems the significance of recuperating cracked connections, encouraging a feeling of solidarity and concordance inside the family.

In addition, the aide underscores the job of ecological cognizance as a worth to be passed down. Really focusing on maturing guardians might include contemplations for the climate, like supportable practices and diminishing waste. Youngsters are urged to pass down the example of natural obligation, cultivating a pledge to economical living that benefits people in the future. By integrating natural cognizance into providing care rehearses, kids add to an inheritance that esteems the significance of safeguarding the planet for the prosperity of all.

Critical to the conversation is the investigation of the likely effect of the illustration of appreciation for social legacy as a worth to be passed down. Maturing guardians might convey rich social practices, and youngsters are urged to pass down the illustration of appreciation for social legacy. By appreciating and saving social practices, dialects, and customs, youngsters add to an inheritance that values variety and the significance of regarding one's social roots.

Additionally, the aide dives into the idea of the meaning of monetary obligation as a worth to be passed down. Really focusing on maturing guardians might include monetary contemplations, and kids are urged to pass down the example of monetary obligation. By overseeing funds wisely and making arrangements for the future, kids add to a heritage that values monetary obligation, giving a steady groundwork to people in the future.

8.3 Encouraging a sense of continuity and connection within the family

In the endearing aide, "Together Through Time: A Youngsters' Manual for Esteeming Maturing Guardians," this part dives into the crucial subject of empowering a feeling of congruity and association inside the family. As kids explore the obligations of really focusing on maturing guardians, encouraging a feeling of congruity turns into a foundation in fortifying the familial bond and safeguarding the tradition of shared encounters, values, and love.

By investigating the manners by which youngsters can empower a feeling of progression and association, this guide highlights the significant effect of these endeavors in making a family embroidery that perseveres through time.

The investigation starts with the acknowledgment of the family story as a focal component in cultivating congruity. The family account includes the common stories, encounters, and customs that characterize the family's aggregate personality. Kids are urged to effectively take part in discussions that rotate around family stories, empowering their maturing guardians to share their background, accounts, and valued recollections. By partaking in the narrating system, youngsters add to a feeling of progression, meshing their own encounters into the texture of the family story and guaranteeing that these accounts are passed down to people in the future.

Besides, the aide stresses the job of family customs in cultivating a feeling of progression. Customs act as ceremonies that tight spot relatives together, making a common feeling of personality and association. Youngsters are urged to effectively partake in and maintain existing family customs while additionally presenting new ones that reverberate with the developing elements of the familial unit. By embracing and sustaining customs, kids add to a feeling of coherence, building up the family's special character and making an extension between the past, present, and future.

Urgent to the conversation is the investigation of the likely effect of reporting family ancestry. Family ancestry is a significant storehouse of recollections, and kids are urged to play a functioning job in reporting the narratives and encounters of their maturing guardians. This can incorporate recording oral accounts, making scrapbooks, or in any event, utilizing computerized stages to protect family recollections. By participating in the documentation of family ancestry, youngsters add to a feeling of progression, guaranteeing that the rich embroidery of the family's past is protected for a long time into the future.

Besides, the aide digs into the idea of recognizing and praising achievements and accomplishments inside the family. Achievements, whether huge or little, mark critical minutes in the family's excursion. Youngsters are urged to communicate appreciation and praise the accomplishments of their maturing guardians, making a culture of affirmation that supports a feeling of progression and association. By perceiving and praising achievements, kids add to a positive family story, featuring the aggregate achievements that have formed the family's common history.

Critical to the conversation is the investigation of the likely effect of making a family heritage project. A family heritage project includes cooperative endeavors to incorporate, sort out, and grandstand the family's ancestry, values, and accomplishments.

Youngsters are urged to start and partake in such undertakings, including different ages all the while. By taking part in a family heritage project, kids add to a feeling of coherence, making an unmistakable portrayal of the family's excursion that can be passed down to people in the future.

Besides, the aide underlines the job of family get-togethers in encouraging a feeling of congruity and association. Family get-togethers give potential open doors to ages to meet up, reinforce bonds, and make enduring recollections. Kids are urged to effectively take part in sorting out and going to family gatherings, working with intergenerational cooperations and guaranteeing that the family stays associated in spite of geological distances. By embracing the custom of family gatherings, kids add to a feeling of progression, making spaces for shared encounters that improve the familial bond.

Urgent to the conversation is the investigation of the likely effect of cultivating intergenerational connections. Intergenerational connections include significant associations between people of various age bunches inside the family. Youngsters are urged to encourage connections with their maturing guardians as well as with grandparents, aunties, uncles, and other more distant family individuals. By sustaining intergenerational connections, kids add to a feeling of congruity, making an organization of help and association that traverses across various ages.

Additionally, the aide digs into the idea of passing down family values and customs through mentorship. Mentorship includes the purposeful exchange of information, abilities, and values starting with one age then onto the next. Kids are urged to look for direction from their maturing guardians and other experienced relatives, gaining from their insight and encounters. By effectively captivating in mentorship, youngsters add to a feeling of progression, guaranteeing that the qualities and customs that characterize the family are passed down with goal and care.

Critical to the conversation is the investigation of the expected effect of integrating family ceremonies into day to day existence. Family ceremonies can be basic yet significant activities that make a feeling of routine and association. Youngsters are urged to effectively partake in and add to everyday or occasional family customs, whether it's a common feast, an assigned family night, or other laid out schedules. By integrating family ceremonies into regular day to day existence, kids add to a feeling of coherence, inserting a feeling of association into the texture of day to day encounters.

Besides, the aide stresses the job of making a family statement of purpose. A family statement of purpose expresses the fundamental beliefs, objectives, and desires that characterize the nuclear family. Kids are urged to team up with their maturing guardians and other relatives in creating a statement of purpose that mirrors the aggregate vision of the family. By making a family statement of purpose, youngsters add to a feeling of congruity, laying out a common system that directs the family's choices and activities.

Urgent to the conversation is the investigation of the likely effect of investigating family ancestry. Family parentage includes following and grasping the heredity and lineage of the family. Youngsters are urged to dig into the investigation of family parentage, revealing accounts of predecessors, figuring out social roots, and valuing the assorted strings that have woven together to make the family's personality. By participating in the investigation of family parentage, youngsters add to a feeling of congruity, perceiving the interconnectedness of past, present, and people in the future.

Besides, the aide dives into the idea of embracing innovation to non-permanent family associations. In the computerized age, innovation offers extraordinary chances to connect generational holes and work with correspondence. Kids are urged to use innovation to remain associated with their maturing guardians, whether through video calls, shared advanced stages, or cooperative web-based projects. By embracing innovation, youngsters add to a feeling of coherence, utilizing present day instruments to reinforce familial associations and guarantee that the family stays joined in spite of actual distances.

Essential to the conversation is the investigation of the possible effect of family instruction drives. Family schooling drives include deliberate endeavors to share information and abilities inside the family. Kids are urged to sort out and partake in Instructive exercises that advance the trading of aptitude and encounters among relatives. By starting family instruction drives, youngsters add to a feeling of congruity, encouraging a culture of long lasting discovering that is gone down through the ages.

Besides, the aide stresses the job of developing a common family character. A common family personality includes an aggregate feeling of having a place and pride in being essential for a similar familial unit. Kids are urged to effectively add to the development of a common family personality by underlining the qualities, customs, and stories that join them. By encouraging a common family character, kids add to a feeling of coherence, making areas of strength for a that ties ages together.

# Chapter 9

## Conclusion

In the piercing excursion illustrated inside "Together Through Time: A Youngsters' Manual for Treasuring Maturing Guardians," the perfection of this humane investigation is a reverberating affirmation of the persevering through force of family securities. Through the interconnected topics of grasping maturing, embracing liabilities, cultivating correspondence, passing down values, and empowering progression, the aide fills in as a compass for kids exploring the mind boggling scene of really focusing on maturing guardians.

As we close this ardent excursion, it is central to think about the all-encompassing message that strings through every part — the significant meaning of family. Maturing guardians, with their abundance of encounters and the inheritance they confer, stand as guides of shrewdness, strength, and love. They address the establishment whereupon the familial embroidery is woven, and this guide support the possibility that their process merits affirmation as well as a festival.

Understanding maturing arises as a foundation, disentangling the intricacies of the maturing system and enlightening the difficulties looked by maturing people. By digging into these viewpoints, kids gain not just a more profound cognizance of their folks' encounters yet additionally an uplifted consciousness of the sympathy and compassion expected in the providing care job.

The ensuing parts change consistently into the domain of obligations and obligations, explaining the complex jobs that kids can play in supporting their maturing guardians. From functional undertakings to daily encouragement, the aide highlights the comprehensive idea of providing care, situating it not as a weight but rather as an equal demonstration of affection and appreciation.

Correspondence, both transparent, arises as a key part in cultivating understanding and exploring the difficulties inborn in focusing on maturing guardians. The aide urges youngsters to embrace successful correspondence systems, guaranteeing that the lines of exchange remain channels of sympathy, empathy, and mutual perspective.

Passing down values expects a focal job, rising above the quick providing care liabilities. The tradition of adoration, regard, care, and different other persevering through standards turns into an immortal present that kids can get and, thus, give to people in the future. This heritage isn't static however unique, advancing as it winds through the unpredictable embroidery of everyday life.

Empowering coherence and association inside the family enhances the familial story, praising achievements, saving practices, and encouraging intergenerational connections. By effectively captivating in the family's aggregate story, kids add to a feeling of congruity that rises above time, making a heritage that reverberations through ages.

As this guide closes, it is fundamental to perceive that esteeming maturing guardians is certainly not a singular undertaking yet an aggregate excursion woven with strings of adoration, understanding, and shared encounters. The repetitive idea of care and backing inside a family is featured, underscoring that the jobs guardians played in kids' lives are reflected in the corresponding consideration gave as guardians age.

The finishing up sections dig into the interconnectedness of ages, underlining the jobs guardians played in shaping the existences of their kids. The aide stresses the recurrent idea of care and backing inside a family, representing the consistent circle of affection and obligation that ties ages together.

Featuring the jobs guardians played in kids' lives repeats a significant truth — the effect of parental direction resounds through time. Youngsters are urged to ponder the basic impact of their folks, perceiving that the qualities ingrained and the illustrations learned add to the versatile texture of the familial bond.

Underlining the recurrent idea of care and backing inside a family fills in as a powerful update that the excursion of really focusing on maturing guardians is definitely not a unidirectional way. Rather, it reflects the correspondence implanted in familial connections, making a bond that rises above ages and supports itself through demonstrations of affection, understanding, and shared liabilities.

Investigating the interconnectedness of ages further supports that the nuclear family is a continuum. As youngsters step into providing care jobs, they become dynamic members in a heritage that ranges both in reverse and forward. The aide energizes an appreciation for the significant interaction between ages, cultivating a feeling of solidarity and coherence that enhances the familial excursion.

The obligations and obligations embraced by youngsters in supporting maturing guardians are raised past simple errands; they become a demonstration of the getting through values that structure the underpinning of the familial bond. The aide highlights that these obligations are not loads yet articulations of adoration, regard, and care, making a proportional cycle that reinforces the familial texture.

Recognizing explicit obligations kids can embrace to help maturing guardians gives commonsense direction, offering a guide for youngsters exploring the intricacies of providing care. From helping with everyday undertakings to offering profound help, every obligation turns into a substantial indication of the affection and appreciation kids hold for their maturing guardians.

Examining the profound and actual requirements of maturing guardians underscores the all encompassing nature of providing care. Youngsters are urged to perceive and answer the complex necessities of their folks, guaranteeing that care stretches out past the actual domain to incorporate profound prosperity and mental help.

Giving instances of little thoughtful gestures that have a tremendous effect builds up the possibility that providing care isn't exclusively about fabulous signals yet additionally about the unpretentious and significant activities that add to a sustaining and strong climate. The aide commends the groundbreaking force of little thoughtful gestures, highlighting their combined effect on the providing care venture.

Successful correspondence arises as a key part in encouraging comprehension and tending to the difficulties of providing care. The aide underscores the significance of transparent correspondence, situating it as a foundation for building trust, settling clashes, and reinforcing the familial bond.

Showing youngsters the significance of transparent correspondence highlights the fundamental job of viable exchange in providing care connections. By ingraining the worth of straightforward correspondence, youngsters add to a climate where considerations, sentiments, and concerns can be communicated transparently, making an establishment for shared understanding and backing.

Giving age-fitting correspondence procedures offers viable experiences into fitting correspondence to suit the extraordinary necessities of maturing guardians. By understanding the subtleties old enough fitting correspondence, youngsters can connect generational holes, guaranteeing that discussions are aware, sympathetic, and helpful for encouraging significant associations.

Tending to normal difficulties in examining delicate points with maturing guardians recognizes the intricacies that might emerge in providing care discussions. The aide furnishes direction on exploring these difficulties with awareness and sympathy, cultivating a climate where troublesome subjects can be drawn closer with compassion and understanding.

Making loved recollections arises as a powerful subject, underscoring the significance of value time in the providing care venture. The aide urges youngsters to effectively participate in exercises that encourage association and euphoria, perceiving that these common minutes become the structure blocks of enduring recollections.

Empowering kids to invest quality energy with their maturing guardians highlights the extraordinary force of shared encounters. By focusing on significant exercises and minutes, youngsters add to a supply of loved recollections that light up the present as well as become getting through treasures in the family story.

Recommending exercises that encourage association and bliss proposes reasonable suggestions for youngsters trying to make significant minutes with their maturing guardians. From straightforward motions to additional intricate excursions, each recommended movement turns into an amazing chance to fortify the familial bond and inject the providing care venture with snapshots of euphoria and association.

Underscoring the benefit of making enduring recollections rises above the quick providing care liabilities, situating memory-production as an inheritance building try. Kids are urged to see each common second as a valuable chance to add to a tradition of affection, bliss, and association that will persevere in the aggregate family story.

Exploring difficulties inside the providing care venture is recognized as a fundamental part of the familial experience. The aide talks about normal difficulties that might emerge and offers bits of knowledge on the most proficient method to approach and beat these impediments with versatility and empathy.

Examining normal difficulties that might emerge in focusing on maturing guardians gives a practical viewpoint on the intricacies of the providing care venture. By recognizing these difficulties, the aide enables youngsters with the information and techniques expected to explore hindrances, encouraging versatility and flexibility notwithstanding challenges.

Giving direction on critical thinking and compromise offers functional instruments for tending to difficulties inside the providing care dynamic. By stressing viable critical thinking methodologies and compromise strategies, the aide furnishes kids with the abilities expected to explore conflicts and cultivate agreeable connections.

Investigating the significance of equilibrium in kids' lives turns into a crucial subject, perceiving that providing care liabilities exist close by different responsibilities and parts of life. The aide empowers a comprehensive methodology that focuses on balance, guaranteeing that kids can satisfy their providing care obligations while likewise keeping an eye on their own prosperity.

Offering methodologies for overseeing providing care liabilities close by different responsibilities gives down to earth direction on accomplishing balance. By consolidating successful using time productively, taking care of oneself practices, and clear correspondence, youngsters can explore the intricacies of providing care while keeping a feeling of balance in different parts of their lives.

Accentuating the meaning of taking care of oneself for kids highlights the significance of focusing on one's prosperity in the midst of the requests of providing care. The aide advocates for taking care of oneself as a fundamental part of keeping up with physical and profound wellbeing, empowering kids to satisfy their providing care jobs with versatility and empathy.

Adjusting liabilities inside the providing care venture is recognized as a nuanced and dynamic undertaking. The aide investigates the difficulties and compensations of adjusting various obligations, perceiving that accomplishing balance requires purposeful endeavors and a promise to both providing care and individual prosperity.

Investigating the interconnectedness of ages turns into a focal topic, featuring the repetitive idea of care and backing inside a family. The aide highlights the jobs guardians played in profoundly shaping the existences of their kids, underscoring that the proportional consideration gave in later years repeats the affection and backing got in before phases of life.

Featuring the jobs guardians played in youngsters' lives repeats a significant truth — the effect of parental direction resonates through time. Kids are urged to consider the basic impact of their folks, perceiving that the qualities ingrained and the illustrations learned add to the versatile texture of the familial bond.

Underscoring the recurrent idea of care and backing inside a family fills in as a strong update that the excursion of really focusing on maturing guardians is definitely not a unidirectional way. Rather, it reflects the correspondence implanted in familial connections, making a bond that rises above ages and supports itself through demonstrations of affection, understanding, and shared liabilities.

Featuring the qualities and illustrations that youngsters can pass down to people in the future typifies the getting through effect of the providing care venture. By ingraining values like compassion, flexibility, appreciation, and open correspondence, youngsters add to an inheritance that shapes the familial embroidery for a long time into the future.

Examining the tradition of affection, regard, and care typifies the quintessence of passing down values inside the setting of appreciating maturing guardians. The aide digs into the significant effect of these qualities, depicting them not as relics of the past but rather as living rules that guide the familial bond, making an embroidery of association that perseveres.

Featuring the qualities and illustrations kids can pass down to people in the future fills in as a directing light inside the excursion of valuing maturing guardians. By digging into these immortal standards, kids add to a relationship that is portrayed by a rich inheritance, reverberating through time and molding the story for a long time into the future.

Empowering a feeling of progression and association inside the family arises as a significant subject, stressing that the excursion of loving maturing guardians is well established in the aggregate encounters, customs, and stories that characterize the nuclear family. By effectively captivating in the safeguarding of family stories, customs, and values, kids add to a feeling of congruity that rises above time.

Encouraging a feeling of coherence includes embracing the lavishness of family stories, customs, and encounters. Kids are urged to effectively partake in the narrating system, maintain family customs, and report the family's ancestry, guaranteeing that the tradition of shared encounters perseveres through ages.

Empowering a feeling of progression and association inside the family fills in as a core value inside the excursion of esteeming maturing guardians. By digging into these deliberate endeavors, youngsters add to a relationship that is described by a rich embroidery of shared encounters, values, and associations. This investigation highlights that cultivating coherence isn't just an affirmation of the past yet a dynamic and continuous work to mesh the strings of familial association into a versatile and getting through texture.

As we explore the pages of "Together Through Time: A Youngsters' Manual for Treasuring Maturing Guardians," the decision carries us to a significant acknowledgment — the excursion of really focusing on maturing guardians isn't simply an obligation; it is an excursion of affection, correspondence, and the immortal bonds that characterize family. The aide, similar to a compass, offers bearing and knowledge, directing youngsters through the intricacies of maturing, providing care, and relational peculiarities.

All things considered, the aide stretches out a solicitation to kids — a challenge to love, appreciate, and effectively take part in the excursion of really focusing on maturing guardians. It highlights that this excursion is certainly not a lone one yet a common encounter that rises above ages. Through figuring out, obligation, correspondence, values, congruity, and association, youngsters become engineers of an inheritance that respects the past, explores the present, and shapes what's to come. The end, similar as the whole aide, repeats a straightforward yet significant truth — that the excursion of valuing maturing guardians is an excursion of the heart, where love, empathy, and shared minutes enlighten the way ahead, together through time.

## 9.1 Summarizing key takeaways

As we ponder the canny and humane excursion spread out in "Together Through Time: A Youngsters' Manual for Loving Maturing Guardians," it becomes fundamental to distil the rich embroidery of shrewdness into key focal points that act as core values for kids exploring the nuanced scene of really focusing on maturing guardians.

Most importantly, the aide highlights the significance of understanding maturing as a crucial mainstay of the providing care venture. By diving into the complexities of the maturing system and recognizing the difficulties looked by maturing guardians, youngsters gain a significant understanding into the profound and actual components of providing care. This grasping structures the bedrock whereupon sympathy, empathy, and powerful help can be fabricated.

A focal topic resounding all through the aide is the all encompassing nature of providing care liabilities. Youngsters are urged to see these obligations not as weights but rather as equal demonstrations of affection and appreciation. From commonsense undertakings to consistent encouragement, the aide underscores that providing care envelops a range of obligations that add to the prosperity of maturing guardians.

Correspondence arises as a key part in the providing care dynamic. The aide advocates for open, fair, and age-suitable correspondence, situating it as a foundation for building trust, settling clashes, and cultivating understanding. Compelling correspondence turns into a channel through which youngsters express sympathy, address difficulties, and guarantee that the providing care venture is set apart by mutual perspective and association.

Passing down values expects a crucial job in molding the tradition of the familial bond. The aide urges kids to embrace and send getting through standards like compassion, versatility, appreciation, and open correspondence. This passing down of values rises above the prompt providing care liabilities, making an inheritance that reverberations through time and adds to the familial embroidery.

Empowering progression and association inside the family turns into a core value that traverses ages. By effectively captivating in the conservation of family stories, customs, and values, kids add to a feeling of progression that rises above time. This purposeful exertion cultivates a familial climate where the past, present, and future are flawlessly woven together, making a versatile and persevering through texture of association.

The aide explores the complexities of making appreciated recollections, featuring the extraordinary force of value time enjoyed with maturing guardians. By empowering kids to take part in exercises that encourage bliss and association, the aide stresses that these common minutes become brief encounters as well as getting through treasures that add to the rich embroidered artwork of family recollections.

Tending to difficulties inside the providing care venture is recognized as an essential part of the familial experience. The aide examines normal difficulties that might emerge and offers bits of knowledge on the most proficient method to approach and beat these snags with strength and sympathy. This affirmation engages kids with the information and methodologies expected to explore troubles and encourage agreeable connections.

Adjusting liabilities turns into a nuanced and dynamic undertaking, perceiving that providing care obligations exist together close by different responsibilities in kids' lives.

The aide empowers an all encompassing methodology that focuses on balance, guaranteeing that kids can satisfy their providing care obligations while likewise watching out for their own prosperity. This fair viewpoint encourages a reasonable providing care dynamic that permits kids to explore their obligations with elegance.

The interconnectedness of ages is a topic woven all through the aide, underlining the recurrent idea of care and backing inside a family. The jobs guardians played in shaping the existences of their kids are reflected in the proportional consideration gave as guardians age. This recurrent excursion highlights the getting through effect of familial connections and the complementary idea of adoration and backing.

Viable critical thinking and compromise are situated as fundamental devices for tending to difficulties inside the providing care dynamic. By accentuating functional procedures, the aide furnishes kids with the abilities expected to explore conflicts and encourage amicable connections. These devices add to a providing care climate where clashes are tended to with sympathy and understanding.

Investigating the significance of equilibrium in youngsters' lives stretches out past providing care liabilities, perceiving the requirement for harmony in different parts of kids' lives. The aide empowers a comprehensive methodology that includes providing care obligations as well as private prosperity, connections, and different responsibilities. This decent viewpoint positions youngsters to explore life's intricacies with strength and beauty.

Passing down values turns into an immortal undertaking, with the aide diving into the tradition of affection, regard, and care. The getting through effect of these qualities is depicted not as relics of the past but rather as living rules that guide the familial bond. This passing down of values makes an embroidery of association that shapes the story of the family for a long time into the future.

Empowering a feeling of congruity and association inside the family fills in as a core value inside the excursion of loving maturing guardians. By diving into purposeful endeavors to safeguard family stories, customs, and values, youngsters add to a relationship described by a rich embroidery of shared encounters, values, and associations. This investigation highlights that encouraging coherence isn't just an affirmation of the past yet a dynamic and continuous work to mesh the strings of familial association into a versatile and getting through texture.

9.2 Reinforcing the idea that cherishing aging parents is an ongoing, fulfilling journey

The overall subject that reverberates all through "Together Through Time: A Kids' Manual for Valuing Maturing Guardians" is the resolute conviction that esteeming maturing guardians is certainly not a static commitment yet a continuous and satisfying excursion. This idea is woven into the texture of every part, filling in as a resonating hold back that highlights the powerful idea of the providing care relationship and the getting through remunerations it brings.

The aide tries to scatter the thought that really focusing on maturing guardians is a limited errand with a reasonable endpoint. All things considered, it urges youngsters to see this obligation as a nonstop and developing excursion that unfurls over the long run. The proportional idea of familial connections is underscored, featuring that the consideration and backing gave to maturing guardians reflect the adoration and direction got in before phases of life.

A vital part of this continuous excursion is the comprehension that maturing is a powerful interaction. The aide digs into the complexities of the maturing system, perceiving that it includes actual changes as well as movements in close to home requirements and viewpoints. By understanding the multi-layered nature of maturing, youngsters are better prepared to adjust their providing care approach, guaranteeing that it remains sensitive to the developing necessities of their folks.

The aide rethinks providing care liabilities as any open doors for association and shared encounters. It stresses that each demonstration of care, whether enormous or little, adds to the continuous account of the familial bond. By effectively captivating in providing care undertakings, kids become dynamic members in the continuous story of their family, cultivating a feeling of progression and association that rises above individual minutes.

Correspondence is situated as a key part in this continuous excursion of valuing maturing guardians. The aide advocates for transparent correspondence as a fundamental apparatus for keeping up with association and understanding. By cultivating a culture of correspondence that is both proactive and responsive, kids add to a climate where the continuous necessities and feelings of maturing guardians are recognized and tended to.

Passing down values is introduced as a getting through heritage that reaches out past prompt providing care undertakings. The aide urges kids to perceive that the qualities imparted by their folks are not static however keep on molding the familial story. This passing down of values turns into a generational trade that improves the continuous excursion of esteeming maturing guardians, making a tradition of affection, regard, and shared standards.

Empowering congruity and association inside the family arises as a core value that supports the possibility of a continuous excursion. By effectively partaking in family customs, recording the family's ancestry, and praising achievements, youngsters add to a feeling of coherence that rises above time. This deliberate exertion encourages a climate where the continuous excursion is set apart by a rich embroidery of shared encounters and values.

The aide dives into the making of treasured recollections for the purpose of mixing bliss into the continuous providing care venture. It underscores that the minutes imparted to maturing guardians, whether through regular exercises or unique events, add to a supply of esteemed recollections. These recollections, woven into the continuous story, become enduring fortunes that enlighten the way ahead.

Tending to difficulties inside the providing care venture is recognized as an indispensable part of the continuous interaction. The aide examines normal difficulties and gives experiences on the best way to explore them with strength and empathy. By moving toward difficulties as any open doors for development and transformation, youngsters add to the continuous improvement of their providing care abilities and reinforce the familial bond.

Adjusting liabilities inside the continuous excursion is perceived as a nuanced and dynamic undertaking. The aide energizes an all encompassing methodology that focuses on providing care obligations as well as private prosperity and different responsibilities. By accomplishing balance, youngsters guarantee that the continuous excursion of loving maturing guardians stays manageable and satisfying, permitting them to explore their obligations with effortlessness.

The interconnectedness of ages is featured as a focal subject that builds up the repetitive idea of care and backing inside a family. The aide highlights that the jobs guardians played in shaping the existences of their youngsters find reverberations in the corresponding consideration gave as guardians age. This interconnectedness positions the continuous excursion as a continuum of adoration, support, and shared encounters that rise above individual lifetimes.

Successful critical thinking and compromise are situated as fundamental apparatuses for exploring the continuous excursion. By underlining functional techniques, the aide outfits youngsters with the abilities expected to address difficulties with compassion and understanding. This critical thinking approach adds to a climate where clashes are seen not as hindrances but rather as any open doors for reinforcing the continuous bond.

Investigating the significance of equilibrium in youngsters' lives stretches out past providing care liabilities to envelop the different features of their reality. The aide empowers a comprehensive methodology that focuses on balance in private connections, taking care of oneself, and different responsibilities.

By accomplishing balance, youngsters guarantee that the continuous excursion of valuing maturing guardians is woven consistently into the texture of their more extensive lives.

Passing down values is depicted as an immortal undertaking that adds to the continuous story of the familial bond. The aide digs into the tradition of affection, regard, and care, stressing that these qualities persevere and shape the continuous excursion of treasuring maturing guardians. This passing down of values turns into a living declaration to the persevering through rules that guide the familial bond across ages.

Empowering a feeling of coherence and association inside the family is introduced as a continuous exertion that requires deliberate commitment. By effectively partaking in family stories, customs, and achievements, youngsters add to a feeling of coherence that rises above individual minutes. This continuous exertion cultivates a climate where the familial excursion is set apart by a solid string of association and shared encounters.

Fundamentally, the aide builds up the possibility that treasuring maturing guardians isn't an errand with a limited endpoint yet a progressing, satisfying excursion that unfurls over the long haul. The recurrent idea of care, the persevering through tradition of values, the making of treasured recollections, and the interconnectedness of ages all add to the extravagance of this continuous account. By embracing the excursion with an open heart, kids become stewards of a heritage that rises above individual lifetimes, making an embroidery of adoration, association, and shared encounters that keeps on unfurling, together through time.

**9.3 Inspiring children to embrace their role in creating a loving and supportive family environment.**

Inside the pages of "Together Through Time: A Youngsters' Manual for Treasuring Maturing Guardians," a rousing story unfurls — one that entices kids to not simply satisfy an obligation but rather to sincerely embrace their part in establishing a cherishing and steady family climate. The aide fills in as a reference point, enlightening the groundbreaking power kids hold in molding the familial story, particularly as their folks age.

The fundamental message is clear: valuing maturing guardians isn't exclusively an obligation however a potential chance to add to a supporting and caring relational intricacy effectively. It provokes youngsters to consider their job to be guardians not as a weight but rather as an opportunity to wind around strings of adoration, understanding, and backing into the multifaceted texture of day to day life.

The aide starts by establishing the vibe, laying out that the excursion of really focusing on maturing guardians is a common undertaking. It highlights the repetitive idea of familial connections, where the consideration gave reverberations the adoration and direction got in before years. This outlining engages kids to see their providing care job not as a detached commitment but rather as a continuation of the complementary bonds that characterize family.

Understanding maturing turns into a foundation, empowering kids to dive into the intricacies of their folks' maturing interaction. By understanding the physical, close to home, and mental aspects, youngsters gain a significant consciousness of the one of a kind difficulties their folks face. This understanding lays the basis for sympathy, encouraging a more profound association that rises above simple providing care undertakings.

The aide's accentuation on correspondence is significant, asking kids to embrace open, genuine, and age-fitting exchange. Powerful correspondence is depicted not simply as the need might arise but rather as a vessel for communicating affection, appreciation, and shared encounters. By effectively captivating in significant discussions, youngsters become designers of a climate where feelings are communicated, comprehended, and responded.

As kids step into providing care jobs, the aide urges them to consider these obligations to be something other than undertakings — they are chances to make loved recollections. The story unfurls like an embroidery, winding around together snapshots of satisfaction, association, and shared encounters. It rouses youngsters to effectively search out exercises that give joy and reinforce the familial bond, adding to a supply of getting through recollections.

The aide recognizes that difficulties are intrinsic in the providing care venture and furnishes direction on exploring them with strength and empathy. By reevaluating difficulties as any open doors for development and understanding, kids are roused to move toward challenges with a feeling of joint effort, strengthening the family climate against possible strains.

Adjusting liabilities is introduced not as a shuffling act but rather as an all encompassing way to deal with life. Youngsters are urged to focus on taking care of oneself, individual connections, and different responsibilities close by their providing care obligations. This equilibrium guarantees that the making of a cherishing and steady family climate reaches out past the quick providing care setting, cultivating generally prosperity.

Passing down values arises as a significant subject, underscoring that the examples gained from guardians are not static however powerful rules that guide the familial bond. Youngsters are urged to effectively epitomize and communicate these qualities, perceiving their job in forming the continuous account of the family. This passing down of values turns into a purposeful demonstration that reinforces the familial establishment.

Empowering coherence and association inside the family turns into a greeting for youngsters to effectively take part in the safeguarding of family stories, customs, and achievements. By looking into the aggregate story, kids add to a feeling of congruity that rises above time. This deliberate exertion encourages a climate where the family's common encounters, values, and customs persevere across ages.

As youngsters take part in the continuous excursion of loving maturing guardians, viable critical thinking and compromise arise as fundamental abilities. The aide engages kids with reasonable techniques for tending to difficulties with compassion and understanding. This critical thinking approach changes clashes into valuable open doors for reinforcing the familial bond, encouraging a strong family climate.

The interconnectedness of ages is praised, featuring that the consideration guardians gave in before years finds reverberations in the equal help given as guardians age. This interconnectedness is depicted as a consistent circle of adoration and direction, underscoring that kids assume a functioning part in supporting the familial bond across various phases of life.

Investigating the significance of equilibrium in youngsters' lives stretches out past providing care liabilities, perceiving the requirement for harmony in different parts of their reality. The aide supports a comprehensive methodology that envelops providing care obligations as well as private prosperity, connections, and different responsibilities. This fair point of view positions youngsters to explore life's intricacies with flexibility and elegance.

Passing down values is depicted as an immortal undertaking that adds to the continuous story of the familial bond. The aide dives into the tradition of affection, regard, and care, underlining that these qualities persevere and shape the continuous excursion of treasuring maturing guardians. This passing down of values turns into a living declaration to the getting through rules that guide the familial bond across ages.

Empowering a feeling of progression and association inside the family is introduced as a continuous exertion that requires deliberate commitment. By effectively partaking in family stories, customs, and achievements, youngsters add to a feeling of coherence that rises above individual minutes. This continuous exertion encourages a climate where the familial excursion is set apart by a whole string of association and shared encounters.